S-01.

2

The Perfect Setting

Menus and Memories from Cincinnati's Taft Museum

Taft Museum
Cincinnati, Ohio

The compilers of this book have taken every precaution to ensure that all recipes have been tried and tested but disclaim any responsibility for errors in quantities or ingredients. Attribution is given to chefs, restaurants, and authors when known.

Additional copies of *The Perfect Setting: Menus and Memories from Cincinnati's Taft Museum* may be obtained by contacting:

Taft Museum Store
Taft Museum
316 Pike Street
Cincinnati, OH 45202

Telephone: (513) 241-0343
Fax: (513) 241-2266
E-mail: taftmuse@fuse.net

First edition

The Taft Museum is the first Fine Arts Fund institution and gratefully acknowledges its continuing support as well as that of the City of Cincinnati. The Ohio Arts Council helped fund this organization with state tax dollars to encourage economic growth, educational excellence, and cultural enrichment for all Ohioans. Museum programs are also funded by an award from the Institute for Museum and Library Services, a federal agency.

On the cover: Belmont (now the Taft Museum) from *Memorial of the Golden Wedding of Nicholas Longworth and Susan Longworth, Celebrated at Cincinnati on Christmas Eve, 1857,* lithograph

All color photographs by Tony Walsh, Cincinnati, OH.

Printed in the USA by

WIMMER
The Wimmer Companies
Memphis
1-800-548-2537

Contents

Preface

In compiling *The Perfect Setting: Menus and Memories from Cincinnati's Taft Museum*, the Taft Museum staff and volunteers sought to provide a new way of appreciating not only the fine arts collection and National Historic Landmark home but also the social history of the families who dwelt there. Much has been written on the paintings, porcelains, decorative arts, and architecture, and this is as it should be. However, many people also want to know about the personalities, tastes, and habits of the former residents: the Baums, Longworths, Sintons, and Tafts.

Each menu, with accompanying recipes, is inspired by a gallery of the Museum as it is currently arranged. Sometimes it is the gallery as a whole, such as the Music Room or Dining Room; other times a single work of art becomes the focus, such as J. M. W. Turner's masterpiece *Europa and the Bull*. A beautiful color image illustrates the inspiration. Accompanying the recipes in each menu, a short essay and historic print or photograph focuses on an aspect of the social history of the house—from Baum's gardens, Longworth's vineyards, Sinton's publishing empire, and the Tafts' political aspirations to accounts of the famous and not-so-well-known visitors who were entertained here between 1820 and 1932.

While inspired by art and history, the recipes in each menu reflect the reality of today's contemporary cook. They use fresh ingredients available in most markets and are designed so that even the novice chef may find success. True to the Taft Museum's legacy, these menus invite readers to make their own history by sharing fine food and conversation with friends and family.

We offer special thanks to the members of the cookbook committee, all volunteers who gave generously of their time and talents, as well as to the local chefs who participated in this project. We also acknowledge the efforts of Catherine L. O'Hara for her editorial work and for writing the essays that accompany each menu. Special thanks as well to John Stevenson, Taft Museum docent, for the historical materials he researched and wrote. His words share equal space with Ms. O'Hara's. Madeleine Lame, Fran Goldman, and Janet Daly are also to be credited for their research efforts. We acknowledge Molly Miller, gourmet cook and former chairwoman of the Docent Corps, for her expertise as recipes editor. This book would not have been possible without the ongoing support of the Taft Museum docents and other volunteers together with the contributions of some of this region's—and the nation's—best chefs.

Phillip C. Long
Director/CEO

Acknowledgments

Cookbook Committee

General Editor: Catherine L. O'Hara
Recipes Editor: Molly Miller
History Editor: Madeleine Lame
History Editor: John Stevenson

Menu Chairs

Vivian Adams-Dobur

Janet Daly

Laura Fidler

Fran Goldman

Eileen Harsnett

Robert F. Kendall

Barbara Kiefer

Barbara Lenhardt

Ruth Lowenthal

Ann Schrimpf

Betsy Schwartz

Testers, Tasters, and Researchers

Charles F. Adams
Vivian Adams-Dobur
Mimi Berning
Greg Braswell
Jean Bruns
Bill Charles
Patricia Charles
Denise Colbert
Robert W. Crawford
Janet Creed
Naomi Dallob
Janet Daly
Ginnie Eaton
Jim Fidler
Laura K. Fidler
Peggy Frank
Bercie Frohman
Jay Gilbert
Mary Gilbert
Fran Goldman
Diane Goodman
Jerry Greene
Kathleen Greene
Carolyn Greenebaum
Linda Harpster
Al Harsnett
Eileen Harsnett
Martha Helmick
Pat Jones

Wes Jones
Joan Keller
Robert F. Kendall
Barbara Kiefer
Florence J. Kiefer
Paula Kirk
Barbara Lenhardt
Ruth Lowenthal
Cindy Marks
Al Masset
Jeanne Masset
Christine Miller
Marvin Miller
Molly Miller
Margaret E. Minton
Scott Minton
Rita Newman
Barbara Noble
Lucy Nowak
Wally Nowak
Joann O'Connell
Mary E. Reed
Rose Reifenberger
Tony Rein
Alis Rule Robinson
Matthew Sabo
Rachel Schrimpf Sabo
Nancy Schild
Alexis Schrimpf

Cyril Schrimpf
Alice Schwartz
Allen Schwartz
Betsy Schwartz
Jane A. Shannon
Marge Sieber
Dorothy Siegel
JoJean Southwick
Steve Suskin
Alice Tateman
Ann Taylor
David Taylor
Carol Terbrueggen
Ralph Terbrueggen
Stephanie Schrimpf Thomson
Douglas Thomson
Joy Tounge
Jane Votel
Tessa Westermeyer
Todd Westermeyer
John van Woensel
Jaye Yorio
Bill Young
Jane Young
Connie Zellner
David Zellner
Ms. Zimmerman's class at
    Sands Montessori School,
    Cincinnati, Ohio

Taft Museum, Cincinnati, Ohio

History and Collections of the Taft Museum

Fine arts, historic house, antique furnishings, the history of some of the region's foremost families—all these are encompassed by Cincinnati's Taft Museum, where masterpieces from the world of art coexist with the architectural elegance of the American Federal period.

Anna Sinton (1852?–1931) and Charles Phelps Taft (1843–1929) began assembling their art collection after 1900, when Mrs. Taft inherited the home from her father, David Sinton (1808–1900). He had purchased the house, then known as Belmont, from the estate of Nicholas Longworth (1782–1863), whose notable artistic legacy was the commission of African American artist Robert Duncanson (1821–1872) to paint a suite of landscape murals in the foyer in about 1850–52. These murals have recently been conserved to restore their original beauty, revealing the masterful hand of the artist from behind the grime of decades. The original owner, entrepreneur Martin Baum (1765–1831), had built the house, then a country villa, by 1820.

Highlights of the Taft Museum collections include paintings ranging from the Old Masters to artists working in Cincinnati during the Tafts' lifetimes. From the incisive portraits by Rembrandt van Rijn, Frans Hals, Thomas Gainsborough, and Sir Joshua Reynolds to the sweeping landscape vistas by J. M. W. Turner and Camille Corot, the quality of the Tafts' selection of paintings from Holland, France, Spain, and Great Britain rivals the collections of major museums in America and abroad.

From America, John Singer Sargent's *Portrait of Robert Louis Stevenson,* James A. McNeill Whistler's *At the Piano,* Frank Duveneck's *Cobbler's Apprentice,* and Henry Farny's famous *Song of the Talking Wire* are each considered among that artist's masterpieces and have been featured as the centerpieces of important exhibitions. As expressed by Paul Provost, vice president and director of American paintings for Christie's in New York City, "The American paintings are particularly fine, with great examples by America's finest 19th-century expatriate painters and great strength in works by Cincinnati artists. Overall it is a unique collection, with choice pictures of the highest quality."

Decorative arts from China, Europe, and America create a homelike ambiance in the Taft Museum galleries. More than 200 examples of 18th-century Qing dynasty Chinese porcelains accent each room with their graceful shapes and intricate designs. It is, according to Chinese export porcelain specialist Becky MacGuire, "as outstanding a collection as that of any small museum in the world." French Renaissance Limoges enamels, 16th- through 18th-century jeweled and enameled watches, Italian maiolica wares and carved rock crystals, and early-19th-century American furnishings by Duncan Phyfe and his contemporaries complete the installations.

As noted by one writer in 1920, "Access to these treasures has always been accorded without stint to those genuinely interested in art history, and the house has frequently been thrown open to members attending any convention in this city. . . . To all it is apparent that there are no Olympian poses in this frame house—only kindliness and good humour" (Brockwell, p. xiii). This spirit holds true today, as the Taft Museum welcomes visitors from Cincinnati and every part of the world for an intimate and extraordinary experience.

Charles Phelps Taft, photograph. Collection of Cincinnati Museum Center, no. B-82-052

Anna Sinton Taft, photograph. Collection of Cincinnati Museum Center, no. B-82-090

Taft Museum Docents

The volunteer docents of the Taft Museum are a group of nearly one hundred dedicated men and women who—day after day, week after week—present school programs, conduct tours for preschoolers through senior citizens, support the Museum's programs and events, and serve as goodwill ambassadors to the community and the world. Collectively, the docents provide nearly ten thousand volunteer hours each year through their activities with students, adults, fundraising efforts, committee work, family programs, continuing education, and clerical support.

The earliest Taft Museum docents came from the Junior League. Three or four women per year studied under then-director Katherine Hanna. In 1972 the first official docent class was initiated, with eighty applicants and forty graduates. New docent classes have continued to join the ranks approximately every two years.

In 1974 the Taft Museum's In School Program was launched with support from the Ohio Arts Council. The program featured docent visits to classrooms with customized suitcases filled with reproductions and learning tools followed by student visits to the Museum to experience the genuine works of art. Four years later the In School Program was recognized for its value to the community with a Post-Corbett Award. The program has undergone changes over the years but continues as a mainstay of the Museum's educational programming.

The role of the docent corps has expanded since the early years to include such specialized programs as sensory tours for people with physical, developmental, or mental disabilities (1997 Post-Corbett Award) and Artists Reaching Classrooms, an intensive program that exposes high school art students to professional artists and to the Taft Museum as a resource for making art. The docents also continue a tradition of fundraising to support educational programs, exhibitions, and scholarships.

The Taft Museum docents consistently exemplify volunteerism at its best through their sense of responsibility, dedication, and loyalty to the Museum. They are a credit to the legacy of founders Anna Sinton and Charles Phelps Taft, who donated their home and art collection to all the people of Greater Cincinnati and who sought to make them accessible to all audiences.

Open House

— Music Room —

Open House
— Music Room —

Menu

Passed Hors d'Oeuvres
Cucumber Watercress Finger Sandwiches
Tomato Monte Carlo Crostini
New Potatoes with Caviar, Bleu Cheese, or Bacon and Sour Cream
Shrimp Wrapped in Snow Peas

Set Hors d'Oeuvres
Belgian Endive Waterlily à la Monet
Bleu Cheesecake
Dim Sum with Hoisin Sauce
Grilled Asian Salmon with Crackers, Sliced Bread Toasts, or Pita Chips
Walnut Mushroom Pâté
Vegetable Polenta

Pastry Table
Strawberry Hazelnut Torte
Chocolate Raspberry Roll with Bittersweet Chocolate Glaze
Carrot Cake with Orange Cream Cheese Icing

MENU CHAIRWOMAN:
Barbara Lenhardt, Taft Museum Special Events Manager

Barbara Lenhardt has been active in the Cincinnati restaurant and catering business for more than 25 years, working with such well-known establishments as Lenhardt's Restaurant and Lenhardt Caterers. Along with recipes for some of the cakes and hors d'oeuvres for which Lenhardt is acclaimed, you will find contributions from a selection of the Taft Museum's "preferred caterers" as well as recipes contributed by several Taft Museum volunteer docents.

Music Room of the Taft Museum

The Music Room has been the site of parties both political and social. From the 50th wedding anniversary of Nicholas and Susan Longworth in 1857 and the wedding of Anna Sinton and Charles Phelps Taft in 1873 to the Sunday afternoon Chamber Music Series that has continued for nearly 50 years—this grand room echoes with the sounds of gatherings past and present. Surrounded by some of the masterpieces of art they collected over the first quarter of the 20th century, Anna and Charles Taft continue to preside from their portraits over the fireplaces, welcoming guests to their open house.

Wedding Bells

On Christmas Eve of 1857, Nicholas and Susan Longworth celebrated their 50th wedding anniversary at their home, Belmont (now the Taft Museum). According to this account from the Cincinnati *Commercial* of December 27, 1857, the "festivities will be remembered by the hundreds who participated in the varied enjoyments of the occasion and will be traditional in the social circles of the city, far in the future of this Christmas eve merry-making. . . . The family pastor, rector of Saint Paul's, pronounced an appropriate prayer and the ring of the Golden Wedding was placed upon the hand of the bride by her great grand-child, Mary L. Stettinius. The company was chiefly remarkable for the large representation of 'old families' of the city, but there was also, of course, a large supply of 'new blood' mingling in the currents of life as it is among us."

Some insight is offered into the contrasting characters of Nicholas and Susan by this account: "The host disappeared early in the evening, having an incorrigible habit of keeping good hours. The hostess, however, gave her guests the pleasure of her society all the evening. . . . A most remarkable and fine looking person is Mrs. Longworth. Bright and original in conversation with the rare gift of expression. . . . Notable as a housekeeper, her dinners and balls made the fine old Pike Street mansion famous" (Chambrun, *Longworth*, p. 102).

Perhaps among the "new blood" that Christmas Eve was David Sinton, a self-made millionaire who was established in Cincinnati by 1847 and would purchase Belmont from the Longworth estate in 1871. Just two years later, on the afternoon of December 4, 1873, Sinton played host to the marriage of his only daughter, Anna (known as Annie), to the blue-blood Cincinnati lawyer Charles Phelps Taft in what was described as "the great social event of 1873 in Cincinnati."

"Annie's white satin gown had a short train, was cut low, and was trimmed with point lace. She wore pearls and diamond jewelry and carried orange blossoms. Charles and she stood under a canopy of evergreens in the fine old mansion on Pike Street. . . . A wedding bell of exotics hung over them as Dr. Skinner, of the Second Presbyterian Church, performed the ceremony" (Ross, pp. 56–58). The *Cincinnati Times and Chronicle* of December 5, 1873, went on to note, "As was expected, everything was conducted in the most elegant style."

View of the Music Room during the residency of Anna Sinton and Charles Phelps Taft, about 1925

Cucumber Watercress Finger Sandwiches

1 (2-pound) package thinly sliced
    white bread

1 English seedless cucumber

1 bunch watercress

1 (8-ounce) package cream cheese,
    softened

2 tablespoons mayonnaise

1 tablespoon seasoned salt

Fresh dill or red bell pepper slivers
    for garnish

- Slice the crusts off the bread and return the slices to the plastic bag to keep them fresh. Cut the cucumber into ⅛-inch slices. Layer cucumber slices in a pan between paper towels to drain.

- Wash the watercress, drain, and discard the larger stems, reserving the leaves. Cream the cream cheese in a food processor. Add mayonnaise and seasoned salt and blend. Add the watercress and blend. Check seasonings and correct if necessary.

- Spread one slice of bread with a thin coating of the watercress spread. Place 4 cucumber slices on top, overlapping if necessary. Top with a slice of bread and cut diagonally into 4 pieces. Place between dampened paper towels to keep the bread from becoming dry. Continue until either the bread or the cucumber slices are gone.

- Garnish each triangle with a small dollop of the cream cheese mixture topped with a sprig of dill or a sliver of red bell pepper.

Yield: 64 sandwiches

Contributor: Barbara Lenhardt

The first step of removing bread crusts and slicing cucumbers may be completed up to one day in advance.

These sandwiches are always a favorite at Taft Museum functions.

Tomato Monte Carlo Crostini

1 thin French baguette

Olive oil

2 tablespoons finely chopped fresh
    garlic

9 Roma tomatoes

Salt and pepper

2 (2-ounce) cans anchovies

20 fresh basil leaves, finely sliced

- Preheat oven to 250°. Slice the bread ¼ inch thick. Place on a cookie sheet, drizzle with olive oil, and sprinkle with garlic. Bake for about 10 minutes until crisp and golden brown. Keep an eye on these as they burn quickly. Allow to cool.

- Slice the tomatoes ¼ inch thick and place one slice on each toast round. Sprinkle with salt and pepper. Drizzle with olive oil. Top with a small slice of anchovy. Garnish with basil and serve.

Yield: about 40 sandwiches

Contributor: Kristin Goltra, food stylist and gourmet cook

New Potatoes with Caviar,
Bleu Cheese, or Bacon and Sour Cream

Small new potatoes

Sour cream

Cooked crumbled bacon, bleu cheese,
    or caviar

- Clean and boil the potatoes until done but not mushy. Drain and cool overnight.

- Cut each potato in half. Using a melon baller or the tip of a teaspoon, scoop a small "bowl" out of each potato. So that the potatoes will remain level when set on a serving tray, slice off a bit of the rounded bottom.

- Fill each "bowl" with sour cream and top with crumbled bacon, bleu cheese, or caviar. If using lumpfish caviar, rinse to remove the coloring and saltiness first and drain on a paper towel.

Contributor: Barbara Lenhardt

No specific quantities are noted for this simple but elegant recipe. Make as many or few as you need. Be fore-warned, your guests will devour them.

Shrimp Wrapped in Snow Peas

Cooked medium shrimp

Homemade or bottled Italian dressing

Snow peas (one per shrimp)

Homemade or bottled cocktail or rémoulade sauce

- Marinate the cooked shrimp in a lightly flavored Italian dressing overnight.
- Trim and remove strings from the snow peas. Blanch briefly in boiling water. Cool immediately by dropping into cold water. Drain.
- Drain the shrimp and wrap each in a pea pod. Secure with a toothpick. Serve with cocktail or rémoulade sauce.

Contributor: Barbara Lenhardt

As with New Potatoes with Caviar, Bleu Cheese, or Bacon and Sour Cream, no specific quantities are given for this easy, make-ahead recipe. You simply need as many snow peas as you have shrimp. Make extras: they are addicting.

Belgian Endive Waterlily à la Monet

1 pound cream cheese, softened

1 tablespoon heavy cream

Assorted dried herbs (dill, thyme, tarragon, basil), to taste

½ teaspoon minced garlic

4 heads Belgian endive

- Mix cream cheese, heavy cream, herbs, and garlic. Form into a ball in the center of a 12- to 14-inch round tray.
- Divide endive into spears. Using the largest spears at the bottom, insert ends into the cheese ball in concentric circles to form a waterlily shape.

Contributor: Judy Larock, former Taft Museum Volunteer Docent

Substitute Boursin cheese for the cream cheese and herbs.

This easy hors d'oeuvre is an artistic addition to any buffet table.

Bleu Cheesecake

1 tablespoon unsalted butter

¼ cup fresh breadcrumbs, toasted

2 tablespoons grated fresh Parmesan cheese

¼ pound bacon, diced

½ medium yellow onion, finely chopped

1 pound cream cheese, softened

¼ pound bleu cheese (Roquefort, Maytag, or Danish)

2 eggs

¼ cup heavy cream

¼ teaspoon salt

⅛ teaspoon hot pepper sauce

Fresh fruit and parsley or watercress for garnish

- Use the butter to grease a 7-inch springform pan. Combine the breadcrumbs and Parmesan and sprinkle over the butter to coat evenly. Chill until ready to fill.

- Cook bacon over medium heat, stirring, until crisp. Drain on paper towels, reserving ½ tablespoon of bacon fat. Sauté the onion in the remaining fat until soft and translucent. Cool.

- Preheat oven to 325°.

- With a food processor or electric mixer, beat together the cream cheese and bleu cheese until smooth. Beat in eggs, cream, salt, and hot pepper sauce. Fold in the bacon and onion. Pour into the prepared pan.

- Set the filled springform pan into a larger baking pan filled with enough hot water to come halfway up the sides of the springform pan. Bake on the middle rack of the oven for 1¼ hours. Cool in the pan of hot water for 1 hour. Chill until ready to serve, garnished with fresh fruit and sprigs of parsley or watercress.

Yield: 15 to 20 cocktail servings

Contributor: Molly Miller, Taft Museum Volunteer Docent

For a big crowd, this recipe can be doubled and baked in a 9- or 10-inch pan.

This recipe was adapted from Marilyn Harris, Cooking with Marilyn, *Cincinnati, 1988.*

Dim Sum with Hoisin Sauce

1 pound ground turkey

⅛ cup soy sauce

2 tablespoons Chinese sesame oil

2 cloves garlic, coarsely chopped

1 tablespoon peeled and coarsely
    chopped fresh ginger root

1 tablespoon honey

2 scallions, cleaned and chopped into
    ¾-inch pieces

1 (50-count) package wonton wrappers

Hoisin sauce

Chopped cilantro or cooked green
    peas for garnish

- Place turkey, soy sauce, sesame oil, garlic, ginger, honey, and scallions in the bowl of a food processor. Mix until smooth.

- Trim the corners off the wonton wrappers to make an octagon. Don't take too much, just the tips. Lay out 6 wrappers and fill each with 1 mounded teaspoon of the turkey mixture. (Keep the remaining wonton wrappers covered to prevent them from drying out.) Pinch the sides of the wrappers together at the top.

- Place the dim sum on the oiled rack of a steamer; do not allow them to touch. Continue making dim sum until the steamer tray is full. Steam for 10 to 12 minutes. Remove from rack and cool. Continue until all the turkey mixture is gone.

- To serve, top each dim sum with a teaspoon of hoisin sauce and either chopped cilantro or a single green pea.

Yield: about 50 dumplings

Contributor: Chateau Pomije

The ungarnished, cooked dim sum can be frozen for later use. To reheat in the microwave, place a dozen or so on a plate, cover with a dampened paper towel, and cook on high for 1 to 2 minutes.

Grilled Asian Salmon with Crackers, Sliced Bread Toasts, or Pita Chips

1 (2- to 3½- pound) side (fillet) salmon, without skin

3 tablespoons black bean garlic sauce

2 tablespoons hoisin sauce

2 tablespoons oyster sauce

2 tablespoons plum sauce

1 tablespoon soy sauce

1 cup orange marmalade

1 tablespoon minced ginger root

½ bunch cilantro, finely chopped

- Place the salmon in a shallow glass baking dish. Combine remaining ingredients and pour over the salmon. Turn to coat both sides of the fish. Cover and let marinate in the refrigerator for 1 or 2 hours.

- Preheat the oven to 350° and start the grill. When the grill is hot, remove the salmon from the marinade (save for later) and lightly wipe off the excess. Place the side of salmon in a wire fish basket and grill for 3 minutes on each side, being careful not to burn the outside.

- Place the grilled salmon in a shallow baking dish, pour the reserved marinade over the fish and bake for 12 to 15 minutes, or until the salmon is just firm to the touch on the thickest part. Remove from the oven and cool.

- Using two metal spatulas, transfer the salmon to a serving tray. To serve either warm or cold, surround the fish with crackers, sliced bread toasts, or pita chips.

Contributor: Elegant Fare

Instead of grilling the salmon, you may broil it in the oven before baking it in the marinade.

Walnut Mushroom Pâté

1½ pounds mushrooms, sliced

1 medium onion, chopped

2 cloves garlic, chopped

11 tablespoons softened butter, divided use

¾ cup toasted walnuts

2 tablespoons Worcestershire sauce

2 tablespoons dry Marsala or port (optional)

¼ teaspoon sugar

1½ teaspoons salt

¼ teaspoon pepper

Chopped parsley for garnish

- Sauté the mushrooms, onion, and garlic in 3 tablespoons of butter until lightly browned and all juice is evaporated.

- Place the mushroom mixture in the bowl of a food processor. Add the remaining butter, toasted walnuts, Worcestershire sauce, optional Marsala or port, sugar, salt, and pepper. Process until smooth. Taste and adjust spices; the flavors will "bloom" so don't over salt.

- Pour the mixture into a greased mold and refrigerate. Before serving, unmold and place on a serving platter and garnish with chopped parsley. Serve with crackers or dark party rye.

Contributor: Richard Golden, The Chafer Caterer

A round bowl makes a handy mold for this simple pâté. If the pâté does not readily come out of the mold, set the mold briefly in a larger bowl of warm water to loosen.

Vegetable Polenta

2 tablespoons butter

1 large onion, chopped

1 green bell pepper, chopped

1 pound mushrooms, sliced

2 cups water

2 cups milk

1 cup cornmeal

1 teaspoon salt

1 large clove garlic, chopped

1 cup grated fresh Parmesan cheese

8 ounces frozen white or yellow corn

1 cup grated Monterey Jack cheese

- Preheat oven to 350°. Melt butter over medium high heat and sauté onion, bell pepper, and mushrooms. Set aside.

- Combine water, milk, cornmeal, salt, and garlic in a heavy saucepan and cook until thick, stirring frequently (about 10 minutes).

- Stir in sautéed vegetables, Parmesan cheese, and corn. Pour mixture into a greased 3-quart rectangular glass baking dish and top with Monterey Jack cheese.

- Bake for 1 hour until bubbly and lightly browned. Allow to cool for 15 minutes before serving. This may also be served at room temperature.

Yield: 12 as an appetizer or 6 as an entrée

Contributor: Barbara Lenhardt

Prepare a half batch in the same size baking dish, allow to cool, and cut into diamonds to serve at room temperature from a platter.

People just can't stop eating this, and they all ask for the recipe. It also microwaves well and makes delicious leftovers.

Strawberry Hazelnut Torte

Cake

1½ cups finely chopped hazelnuts

4 rounded tablespoons flour

8 egg whites

1 cup granulated sugar

8 egg yolks

- Measure and assemble near the electric mixer all the ingredients so they can be added with no time lost. Preheat the oven to 350°. Combine the hazelnuts and flour.

- Place the egg whites in the mixing bowl. Whip at high speed until they form stiff peaks. Add the sugar. Immediately reduce the speed to medium and add the egg yolks. Reduce the speed to low and add the nut and flour mixture, mixing a few seconds. Remove the bowl from the mixer and using a rubber spatula, hand fold lightly to mix any remaining ingredients. Do not overmix, as the air in the batter makes it rise.

- Pour the batter into 2 lightly greased and floured 9-inch round cake pans. Bake for 35 minutes, or until the sides pull away from the pan and the top is lightly browned and springy to the touch. Allow to cool slightly. Run a knife around the pans and remove each layer to a cooling rack.

- When completely cooled, cut each layer in half horizontally using a long thin serrated bread knife.

Filling

1 pound unsalted butter, softened

1½ cups powdered sugar

1 teaspoon vanilla

Juice of 1 lemon or 1 tablespoon fruit juice

1 quart strawberries, sliced

- Beat butter, powdered sugar, vanilla, and lemon or fruit juice together using an electric mixer. Add more powdered sugar if mixture is too thin.

- Spread one layer of cake with buttercream and top with sliced strawberries. Continue this process for the second and third layers. Place the final layer on top. Ice top and sides with remaining buttercream. Garnish top with fruit.

- Chill, serve, and stand back to accept the compliments.

Yield: 12 servings

Contributor: Barbara Lenhardt

Sliced bananas may be substituted for the strawberries. Brush the top layer of bananas with lemon juice to keep them from browning.

Chocolate Raspberry Roll with Bittersweet Chocolate Glaze

Cake

2 rounded tablespoons unsweetened cocoa

4 rounded tablespoons flour

9 egg whites

1 cup granulated sugar

9 egg yolks

1 teaspoon vanilla

- Measure and assemble near the electric mixer all the ingredients so they can be added with no time lost. In addition, be sure that the mixer bowl and beaters are grease free, as grease will prevent the egg whites from forming stiff peaks. Preheat the oven to 350°. Put the cocoa through a sieve and combine with the flour.

- Beat egg whites at high speed until they form stiff peaks. Immediately add the sugar. Reduce speed to medium and add the egg yolks and vanilla. Reduce speed to low and add the cocoa mixture, mixing an additional few seconds while scraping the sides with a rubber spatula. Remove the bowl from the mixer and hand fold with the spatula until all the ingredients are blended. Do not overmix, as the air in the batter makes it rise.

- Pour the batter into a jelly-roll pan or cookie sheet with sides that has been lined with parchment or waxed paper.

- Bake for 35 to 45 minutes until the sides of the cake pull away from the pan and the top is springy to the touch. Allow to cool for 10 minutes.

- Beginning with a long side of the rectangle, roll the cake with the parchment on. Allow to cool completely, then unroll and remove the parchment paper. It should come off easily, because steam trapped inside loosens the paper. Place the unrolled cake on a large cooling rack placed over a cookie sheet.

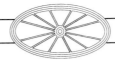

Filling

1 pint heavy cream

1 cup powdered sugar

1 teaspoon vanilla

½ cup seedless raspberry preserves

- Whip the cream with powdered sugar and vanilla until stiff. Gently fold in raspberry preserves until well blended.

- Fill the cake with three quarters of the flavored whipped cream and roll the two long sides together so that they touch, forming one continuous circle around the filling. Leave the filled roll on the rack over the cookie sheet, seam side down.

Bittersweet Chocolate Glaze

4 ounces unsweetened baking chocolate

1 tablespoon butter

½ pound powdered sugar

Hot coffee

Grated chocolate

- Melt the chocolate in a glass bowl in the microwave or over hot water in a double boiler. In a mixing bowl, stir the butter into the chocolate until it melts. Beat in the powdered sugar. Use a small amount of hot coffee to create a glaze of medium thickness that can be spread lightly onto the roll. Add more powdered sugar as needed.

- Spread glaze over the roll. The pan under the rack will catch any drips. After glazing the roll, use two spatulas to move it to a serving tray. Put the remaining whipped cream in a pastry bag and decorate the top and sides of the roll. Sprinkle with grated chocolate. Refrigerate until serving time.

- To serve, use a thin knife dipped in hot water to cut the roll into slices, dipping the knife in the water between each slice. Use a light sawing motion with the knife handle angled up to avoid squashing the roll while slicing.

Yield: 18 to 20 servings

Contributor: Barbara Lenhardt

For Chocolate Mocha Roll, substitute ¼ cup instant coffee dissolved in ¼ cup hot water for the raspberry preserves in the whipped cream filling.

This cake was served amid many "bravos" to patrons at Cincinnati Playhouse in the Park. Now, for an encore, reprise it in your own house.

Carrot Cake with Orange Cream Cheese Icing

Carrot Cake

3 eggs

1 cup white sugar

1 cup brown sugar

¾ cup vegetable oil

¾ cup buttermilk

2 teaspoons vanilla

2 cups flour

2 teaspoons baking soda

½ teaspoon salt

2 teaspoons cinnamon

1 (8-ounce) can crushed pineapple, drained

2 cups grated carrot

1 cup grated coconut

½ cup walnuts

½ cup raisins

- Preheat oven to 350°. In the bowl of an electric mixer, cream eggs, white sugar, and brown sugar. Beat in vegetable oil, buttermilk, and vanilla.

- Sift together flour, baking soda, salt, and cinnamon. Mix dry ingredients into batter until smooth. Stir in pineapple, carrots, coconut, walnuts, and raisins.

- Grease and flour two 9-inch round cake pans or one 3-quart rectangular glass baking dish. Pour in batter and bake for 45 to 60 minutes. Allow round cakes to cool in pans for 10 minutes before removing to a wire rack. Cool rectangular cake in pan.

Orange Cream Cheese Icing

4 ounces unsalted butter, softened

8 ounces cream cheese, softened

2 cups powdered sugar

Juice and zest of 1 orange

1 teaspoon vanilla

- In the bowl of an electric mixer, cream the butter and cream cheese. Add powdered sugar, orange juice and zest, and vanilla. Beat until smooth. Add more powdered sugar if needed to make the icing thicker for spreading.

- For a layer cake, ice the tops and sides of the two rounds. For a sheet cake, ice the top of the rectangular cake. Serve.

Yield: 12 to 16 servings

Contributor: Barbara Lenhardt

This citrus version of the classic is a perennial favorite.

Vive la France

An Elegant French Dinner Party for Eight

— Dining Room —

Vive la France
An Elegant French Dinner Party for Eight
— Dining Room —

Menu

Appetizer
Filet de Saumon Poêle aux Crevettes et Moules
(Sautéed Fillet of Salmon with Shrimp and Mussels)

Entrée
Côté de Veau Sautée au Vin de Bourgogne
(Sautéed Veal Chop in Burgundy Wine Sauce)

Haricots Verts en Panier de Tomate
(French Green Beans in a Tomato Basket)

Caissette de Pomme de Terre aux Petits Légumes
(Minced Vegetables Baked in a Potato Shell)

Salad
Salade de Mesclun avec Noisette et Vinaigre de Framboise
(Mixed Greens with Hazelnut Oil and Raspberry Vinegar Dressing)

Dessert
Oranges et Fraises au Sabayon de Liqueur d'Orange
(Oranges and Strawberries in Orange Liqueur Sabayon)

MENU CHAIRWOMAN:
Ann Schrimpf, Taft Museum Docent

CHEF:
Georges Haidon

Currently consultant to Cincinnati's Queen City Club, Georges Haidon served as executive chef at the five-star Maisonette for 23 years before retiring in 1994. Born in Belgium, he studied the culinary arts there before embarking on a career that has spanned more than 50 years and has included such diverse assignments as hotels, restaurants, ships, and airlines. Although officially retired, he remains active by consulting for some of Cincinnati's finest culinary establishments.

Charles-François Daubigny (French, 1817–1875), *Evening on the Oise,* **1863, oil on canvas, h. 39¼ x w. 78¾ in. Bequest of Mr. and Mrs. Charles Phelps Taft**

The Dining Room is home to landscapes—including Jean-François Daubigny's masterpiece *Evening on the Oise*—by the French Barbizon School of artists who worked around the forest of Fontainebleau and the village of Barbizon during the mid-19th century. The inspiration for the later impressionists, the Barbizon artists rejected academic formulas and took their paint boxes into the woods and meadows to record what they saw. These green and misty scenes of forest, field, and river provide the inspiration for this elegant French dinner party.

The Cincinnati Wine Country

What would a fine French meal be without wine? During the mid-19th century, Cincinnati had established itself as a major wine-producing region with Nicholas Longworth, a lawyer, abolitionist, and horticulturist, leading the way with vineyards that stretched from his home on Pike Street (now the Taft Museum) far into what are now the neighborhoods of Mount Adams, Walnut Hills, and Hyde Park.

According to an 1857 report on the state of viticulture in Cincinnati, "The early and continued efforts of Nicholas Longworth, Esq., induced many of the farmers of the country to turn their attention to the cultivation of the grape, . . . and we may now safely predict, that the Ohio Valley is to be the rival of the vine-growing regions of Europe; nor is the time far distant when the Catawba and Herbemont wines of Hamilton county will ornament the tables of the aristocracy of the old world" (Cary, n.p.). The very sobriquet "The Queen City" comes from Henry Wadsworth Longfellow's ode to Mr. Longworth's wine: "This song of the vine,/This greeting of mine,/The winds and the birds will deliver/To the Queen of the West,/In her garlands dressed,/On the banks of the beautiful river."

An early guidebook to Cincinnati provides this description of Longworth's winemaking operation: "The Longworth wine-cellar, one of the established lions of the city, cheers the thirsty soul of man. There we had the pleasure of seeing, by a candle's flickering light, two hundred thousand bottles of wine, and of walking along subterranean streets lined with huge tuns, each of them large enough to house a married Diogenes, or to drown a dozen Dukes of Clarence, and some of them containing five thousand gallons of the still unvexed Catawba. It was there that we made acquaintance with the 'Golden Wedding' champagne, the boast of the late proprietor, an acquaintance which we trust will ripen into an enduring friendship. If there is any better wine than this attainable in the present state of existence, it ought, in consideration of human weakness, to be all poured into the briny deep" (Atlantic Monthly, p. 241).

View of the Dining Room during the residency of Anna Sinton and Charles Phelps Taft, about 1925

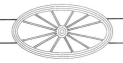

Filet de Saumon Poêlé aux Crevettes et Moules
(Sautéed Fillet of Salmon with Shrimp and Mussels)

Mussels and Sauce

2 tablespoons butter

1 medium onion, diced

2 celery ribs, diced

4 pounds mussels

1 cup water

Salt and pepper

Heavy cream

- Melt butter over medium heat in a large Dutch oven. Add onion and celery and sauté for 3 or 4 minutes without browning. Add mussels and water. Season with salt and pepper. Cover and simmer until the mussels open. Remove from heat.

- Strain the cooking liquid. Shell mussels and reserve. Return the cooking liquid to the pan and boil to reduce volume by half. Add the same amount of heavy cream and reduce again until the sauce thickens slightly. Check seasonings and strain again, if necessary. Return the shelled mussels to the pan and keep warm.

Salmon and Shrimp

8 (4-ounce) center-cut salmon fillets

16 peeled and deveined shrimp (10 count)

Salt and pepper

2 tablespoons butter

2 tablespoons chopped parsley

- Season the salmon and shrimp with salt and pepper. Melt butter in a heavy skillet. When butter foams, add the salmon fillets and cook for 5 minutes on each side. Remove salmon from pan.

- Add shrimp to same pan and cook 2 minutes on each side. Remove shrimp and cut in half lengthwise.

- Place one salmon fillet in the center of each dinner plate. Arrange 4 shrimp halves on top of each salmon fillet. Arrange mussels around the salmon. Spoon the sauce all around. Garnish with a sprinkling of chopped parsley.

Yield: 8 servings

The mussels can be cooked, shelled, and refrigerated in their cooking liquid the day before serving.

This dish makes a lovely luncheon or light supper entrée when paired with a salad. The mussels and sauce are also delicious served over pasta.

Côté de Veau Sautée au Vin de Bourgogne
(Sautéed Veal Chop in Burgundy Wine Sauce)

Veal Stock

- 2 tablespoons vegetable oil
- 1 pound veal trimmings
- 1 medium carrot, sliced
- 2 celery ribs, sliced
- 1 medium onion, sliced
- 1 ripe tomato, sliced
- Pinch thyme
- 1 bay leaf
- 1 whole clove
- Water
- Salt and pepper

- In a large heavy skillet, heat vegetable oil over medium high heat. Add the veal trimmings, sliced vegetables, thyme, bay leaf, and clove. Brown well.
- Cover with water and bring to a boil. Simmer for 2 hours. Strain the liquid and remove the fat from the top with a ladle. Season with salt and pepper. To yield 4 cups of stock, return to a boil and reduce if necessary.

Burgundy Wine Sauce

- 2 tablespoons butter
- 3 shallots, chopped
- 1 teaspoon cracked pepper
- 1 cup Burgundy wine

- Melt butter over medium-high heat. Add shallots and sauté until translucent. Add pepper and wine. Bring to a boil to reduce to ½ cup (10 minutes).
- Add the veal stock and reduce again to about 2 cups (15 to 20 minutes).

Veal Chops

- 2 tablespoons butter
- 8 (9- to 10-ounce) veal chops

- Melt butter over medium high heat. Sauté veal chops on both sides; they should be slightly pink inside. Remove from pan.
- Pour off excess butter and pour prepared sauce into the pan. Boil, strain, and keep warm until serving time.

Yield: 8 servings

For an easy shortcut, substitute 2 cups of canned chicken broth and 2 cups of canned beef broth for the veal stock. The veal stock may also be prepared the day before and refrigerated until it is time to add it to the wine sauce.

Haricots Verts en Panier de Tomate
(French Green Beans in a Tomato Basket)

8 small tomatoes, approximately
   3 inches in diameter

Salt and pepper

1½ pounds of French green beans

2 shallots, chopped

4 tablespoons butter

2 tablespoons chopped parsley

- Place tomatoes stem side down on a cutting board. To form the handle of the tomato basket, make 2 vertical cuts, ½ inch apart and 1½ inches deep. Make 2 horizontal cuts on each side of the tomato to meet the vertical cuts. Remove the wedges. Carefully cut out the inside of the handle, leaving ¼ inch of flesh. If it is any thinner, it will collapse. Remove the seeds and half of the remaining flesh from the bowl of the basket. Sprinkle with salt and pepper.

- Trim the green beans and cut to 3½-inch lengths. Cook in salted water until still slightly firm. Meanwhile, sauté the shallots in butter until translucent, without browning. Add beans and continue cooking for 3 to 5 minutes. Add parsley and keep warm.

- Lay the green beans lengthwise in the tomato baskets. Before serving, heat in the oven at 375° for 3 minutes.

Yield: 8 servings

Use a grapefruit spoon to remove seeds and flesh neatly and easily from the tomatoes. If French green beans are not available, substitute regular green beans.

This side dish looks spectacular and is very easy. It makes a great addition to your holiday table.

Caissette de Pomme de Terre aux Petits Légumes

(Minced Vegetables Baked in a Potato Shell)

8 medium baking potatoes

Salt and pepper

2½ tablespoons butter, divided use

1 cup each, ¼-inch diced carrots, celery, leeks, and turnips

Water

2 tablespoons grated fresh Parmesan cheese

- Preheat oven to 425°.

- Peel the potatoes into a rectangular shape, roughly 2 inches wide by 4 inches long by 1½ inches high. Using a sharp knife, make a ¾ inch deep incision ¼ inch inside the top perimeter. Use a melon baller to make a ¾ inch deep cavity inside the incision. Season with salt and pepper. Melt 1½ tablespoons butter and brush over potatoes. Bake for 25 minutes.

- Melt the remaining tablespoon of butter in a large skillet over medium heat. Add the diced vegetables, moistened with a little water. Cook slowly without browning. Remove the vegetables while still slightly firm. There should be no liquid remaining. Season with salt and pepper to taste and stir in the Parmesan.

- Fill each potato with the vegetable mixture and reheat at 375° for 3 to 5 minutes before serving.

Yield: 8 servings

Salade de Mesclun avec Noisette et Vinaigre de Framboise

(Mixed Greens with Hazelnut Oil and Raspberry Vinegar Dressing)

2 egg yolks

⅓ cup raspberry vinegar

Salt and pepper

1 cup hazelnut oil

2 tablespoons chopped chives

2 tablespoons chopped parsley

Mixed greens (Bibb, red oak leaf, romaine, curly endive, etc.)

Cherry tomatoes and radishes (optional)

- In a small bowl, mix the egg yolks and vinegar. Add salt and pepper. Slowly add the oil, whisking constantly to make a smooth dressing. Stir in chives and parsley.
- Wash and dry the mixed greens. Pile in the center of each plate. Garnish with cherry tomatoes and radishes, if desired. Top with dressing.

Yield: 8 servings

Many supermarkets carry prewashed salad mix.

This dressing is light and nutty. The salad makes a fine light luncheon accompanied by soup and crusty French bread.

Oranges et Fraises au Sabayon de Liqueur d'Orange

(Oranges and Strawberries in Orange Liqueur Sabayon)

8 ounces fine sugar

12 egg yolks

1 cup orange juice

1 cup orange-flavored liqueur

8 oranges

1 quart strawberries, hulled

Powdered sugar

- In a small bowl, whisk the fine sugar and egg yolks until the mixture whitens slightly. Dilute with orange juice and liqueur.

- Pour the sabayon mixture into the top of a double boiler over boiling water, and whisk rapidly until it is firm and frothy. Remove top of double boiler from heat and place directly into a bowl of ice water, whisking constantly until cold.

- Peel and section the oranges. Use a sharp knife to remove the membranes and any seeds from the sections.

- To serve, pour sabayon into the well of each dinner plate, being careful not to go over the rim. Place one whole strawberry in the center of the plate. Arrange orange slices radiantly around the strawberry and sliced or halved strawberries between the orange sections. Sprinkle with powdered sugar just before serving.

Yield: 8 servings

Use a tea strainer or small sifter to elegantly and easily sprinkle the powdered sugar.

This rich and fruity dessert is a stunning end to a special meal.

Five Heavenly Foods

A Chinese Buffet

— *China Closet* —

Five Heavenly Foods
A Chinese Buffet
— *China Closet* —

Menu

Drunken Chicken

Spicy Ginger Beef

Marinated Cutlets

A Platter of Two Deliciousnesses

Jump-into-Your-Mouth Chinese Vegetables

MENU CHAIRWOMAN:
Betsy Schwartz, Taft Museum Docent

CHEF:
Charles E. Bolton

Charles E. Bolton is president of Federation Antiques, which specializes in period antiques, interior design, and fine art and was founded in Cincinnati in 1980. Menu Chairwoman Betsy Schwartz describes him as "a man for all seasons," someone who does many things well. One of those things is cooking, which Mr. Bolton says, he has "been wild about since the age of 14." We know you will be wild about his Five Heavenly Foods.

Phoenix Ewer, **Ming dynasty (1368–1644), about 1570–80, porcelain with silver-gilt mounts (Nuremberg, about 1600, with later additions), h. 11¾ in.**
Bequest of Mr. and Mrs. Charles Phelps Taft

*M*odeled after China closets in the great homes of England, this former pantry houses porcelains from China. Dating from the Tang dynasty (618–907) through the Qing dynasty (1644–1911), this choice selection collected over 25 years includes the rare Ming dynasty *Phoenix Ewer,* set with silver German mounts. The beautiful plates, saucers, dishes, teapots, brushwashers, figures, animals, and vases—many of which were made for export to the West during the early 1700s—provide a capsule of Chinese design motifs and history as well as inspiration for today's popular Chinese cookery.

Parties and More Parties

The big house on Pike Street, inaugurated in 1825 by a house warming given by its first occupant, Martin Baum, remained the place for parties in Cincinnati throughout its history as a private dwelling—continuing that reputation today through Taft Museum functions and private affairs.

Nicholas Longworth continued the tradition established by Baum. As early as 1829, the year he bought the house, in "the *Retrospect of Western Travel* we read about an 'elegant party at a splendid house.' The host's ruling passion bids fair to be a blessing to the city. He employs four gardeners and toils in the grounds with his own hands. Between the garden and the hills extend his vineyards; in this setting the visitor 'met among many other guests one of the judges of the Supreme Court, a member of Congress and his lady, two Catholic priests, Judge Hall, the popular writer, with divines, physicians, lawyers, merchants and their families. The spirit and superiority of the conversation were worthy of the people assembled' " (Chambrun, *Cincinnati*, p. 149).

Some years later on May 18, 1841, "Nicholas Longworth gave a general party in honor of his son's marriage. The house was crowded and at about 10 o'clock their lovely garden sprang up in one blaze of lights, a beautiful illumination; it was like enchantment, and a glowing imagination could have fancied the white dresses that were seen ever and anon winding among the trees to be sprites holding their evening revels" (Chambrun, *Cincinnati*, p. 203).

While David Sinton, the next owner of the house, was not inclined toward parties, his daughter, Anna Sinton Taft, was. In 1883, her husband, Charles, "was inclined to be critical as he studied the Pike Street household bills at this time. Annie had annoyed her father, too, with a party she had given for 560 guests in honor of Sir John Coleridge, Chief Justice of Queen's Bench. It always gave her pleasure to snare a visiting icon. Her father footed the bills, but complained bitterly. Will [her brother-in-law William Howard Taft] took another view of this and wrote to his mother: 'The house is so well suited to entertaining and he is so rich that it is eminently proper that he should entertain the city's guests.' . . . Willful, impulsive, pretty and full of high spirits, Annie was an affectionate wife, a conscientious mother, and she created an aura of gaiety around her" (Ross, p. 79).

True to her nature, when "Charles was nominated by acclamation [to run for Congress in 1894], Annie immediately gave a party and served punch 'strong enough to curl your hair.' The drawing room had been done over and she drew Will's attention to the stunning chandelier from Vienna that his mother had given her. They agreed that it looked well in the Pike Street setting" (Ross, p. 119).

A. O. Elzner, *Sketch of the Sinton Residence*, 1882

Drunken Chicken

1 (5- to 6-pound) whole chicken

4 to 5 tablespoons kosher salt, to taste

1½ cups chicken broth, or more as needed

3 cups Shaohsing (rice wine), or more as needed

Minced cilantro or parsley for garnish

- Place the whole chicken in a deep dish that will fit in the top of a steamer over boiling water. Cover and steam until chicken is tender, about 1¼ to 1½ hours. Remove chicken and allow to cool. Cut cooled chicken into pieces.

- Spoon salt onto waxed paper and generously salt the chicken pieces one at a time by hand. Place the salted chicken in a bowl, cover with waxed paper and tightly fitted lid and let stand in the refrigerator for 6 to 8 hours.

- Combine the chicken broth and wine. Pour enough over chicken just to cover, reserving any remainder. Cover the chicken again and refrigerate for at least 14 hours and up to 3 days.

- Before serving, either use a cleaver to chop the chicken into bite-sized morsels or debone. Arrange on a platter and sprinkle with the reserved wine mixture. (If no wine mixture remains, combine an additional ⅓ cup wine with ⅓ cup broth and pour over chicken.) Garnish with cilantro or parsley.

Yield: 8 main dish servings or 12 as part of a buffet

Drunken Chicken makes an excellent base for Chinese chicken salad.

While often served hot as a main dish, this version of Drunken Chicken is served cold as an appetizer or part of a large buffet.

Spicy Ginger Beef

1 pound flank steak

2 teaspoons cornstarch

1 tablespoon dark soy sauce

1½ teaspoons vegetable oil, plus 1 cup, divided use

½ cup finely shredded fresh ginger

1 teaspoon kosher salt

½ teaspoon sugar

1 tablespoon dry sherry or Shaohsing (rice wine)

2 cups tightly packed cilantro leaves

- Slice the beef across the grain as thinly as possible. (Chill in the freezer for half an hour for easier slicing.) In a mixing bowl, combine cornstarch, soy sauce, and 1½ teaspoons oil. Add the sliced beef and stir to coat. Cover and set aside.

- In a small bowl, combine the ginger and salt. Let stand 30 minutes. Drain and squeeze to eliminate accumulated moisture.

- In a wok, heat 1 cup of oil over high heat until smoking, then remove from heat. Add the beef when the oil has cooled just a bit and return to heat. Cook at medium high, stirring constantly until the pieces separate and have lost most of their red color, approximately 2 to 3 minutes. Do not overcook, or the meat will become tough. Drain well, discarding all but 2 tablespoons of the oil. Set beef aside.

- Blend the sugar and sherry and set aside.

- Reheat the remaining 2 tablespoons of oil in the wok. Add the ginger and cook, stirring, about 15 seconds. Add the beef and cook about 15 seconds longer. Stir in the cilantro and cook about 10 seconds. Add the wine mixture and stir to blend. Serve immediately.

Yield: 8 main dish servings or 12 as part of a buffet

Much of the preparation can be done in advance; the final cooking goes very quickly.

This dish is best served very hot.

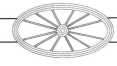
Marinated Cutlets

8 slices center-cut pork loin (½ inch thick)

8 tablespoons soy sauce

½ teaspoon cayenne pepper

¼ teaspoon monosodium glutamate (optional)

3 teaspoons Chinese sesame oil

1½ teaspoons sugar

¼ cup cornstarch

¾ cup vegetable oil

- Place the cutlets on a flat surface and pound lightly with the back of a cleaver, being careful not to break the meat. Use a sharp knife to lightly score each piece on both sides.

- Combine soy sauce, cayenne, monosodium glutamate, sesame oil, and sugar and stir until sugar is dissolved. Pour the marinade into a flat dish and add the cutlets in a single layer. Let stand about 1 hour, turning the cutlets occasionally.

- Drain cutlets. Using about 1½ teaspoons cornstarch, sprinkle a cutlet, rubbing it in and lightly coating both sides. Repeat for the remaining cutlets.

- Pour the vegetable oil into one or two skillets, as necessary, to a depth of about ¼ inch over medium to medium high heat. When the oil is hot, add the cutlets in a single layer. Cook uncovered about 7 minutes on each side. When golden brown, drain and remove to a warm platter. Cover lightly with foil until ready to serve. Serve at room temperature, surrounded by hot Jump-into-Your-Mouth Chinese Vegetables.

Yield: 8 main dish servings or 12 as part of a buffet

Serve cutlets with any of several savory condiments, such as Chinese hot mustard, plum sauce, or black bean sauce, all of which are readily available at Chinese markets and many supermarkets.

A Platter of Two Deliciousnesses

12 ounces medium shrimp, shelled and deveined

12 ounces large sea scallops

1½ pounds firm, slender asparagus spears

3 tablespoons dry sherry

2 tablespoons cornstarch

½ cup vegetable oil, divided use

3 tablespoons Chinese sesame oil

Salt and pepper

- Wash shrimp thoroughly and pat dry. Slice scallops horizontally into the thinnest slices possible. Clean asparagus, remove woody ends, and slice diagonally into 2-inch pieces. Combine sherry and cornstarch.

- In a wok, heat ¼ cup vegetable oil until smoking. Remove from heat and allow to cool for 30 seconds. Slide the scallops into the oil one at time using a wooden spatula. Return to the heat and cook, using the spatula to keep the slices separate, for 2 to 3 minutes until opaque. Drain in a sieve. Pat scallops dry on paper towels and reserve.

- Heat the remaining ¼ cup oil in the wok. When very hot, add the asparagus and cook, stirring constantly, for 3 minutes. Add the shrimp and cook 3 minutes longer. Return the scallops to the wok and drizzle sesame oil over the mixture. Cook 1 minute longer, stirring until thoroughly mixed. Season with salt and pepper, if desired.

- Use a slotted spoon to remove the mixture to a warmed serving platter. Return the wok to the heat. Add the sherry mixture and stir until slightly thickened and transparent. Pour over platter. Serve immediately.

Yield: 8 main dish servings or 12 as part of a buffet

Jump-into-Your-Mouth Chinese Vegetables

1 large bunch scallions (15 to 20)

2 large red bell peppers

1 large head bok choy

1 (6- to 8-ounce) can baby corn

1 (6-ounce) can sliced water chestnuts

½ cup vegetable broth

2 tablespoons Shaohsing (rice wine) or dry sherry

4 tablespoons light soy sauce

2 teaspoons cornstarch

4 to 6 tablespoons vegetable oil

- Prepare all vegetables. Slice scallions into 2-inch pieces. Clean and seed bell peppers, and cut into 1-inch squares. Wash and dry bok choy. Cut stalks into 2-inch slices, and tear leaves into bite-sized pieces. Drain, rinse, and dry corn and water chestnuts.

- Stir together broth, wine or sherry, soy sauce, and cornstarch. Set aside.

- In a large wok, heat 4 tablespoons of oil until very hot. Add scallions, bell peppers, and bok choy. Cook, tossing with a wooden spoon, until the leafy parts of the bok choy are wilted, about 4 minutes. Add additional oil 1 tablespoon at a time, if needed.

- Add baby corn and water chestnuts and continue cooking 2 minutes, stirring constantly.

- Add the reserved stock mixture and continue cooking, folding the vegetables into the liquid until all are coated, about 1 minute. Serve immediately.

Yield: 8 main dish servings or 12 as part of a buffet

A Presidential Repast

Dinner from America's Heritage

— President's Room —

A Presidential Repast
Dinner from America's Heritage
— President's Room —

Menu

Scalloped Oysters

*Mixed Greens in Vinaigrette**

*Roast Pork**
Mashed Potatoes and Turnips
Corn Pudding
Lemon-Glazed Carrots and Rutabagas

Trifle
Apple Crisp

*Use your favorite recipe to prepare these dishes.
All other recipes are provided on the following pages.

MENU CHAIRWOMAN:
Janet Daly, Taft Museum Docent

CHEF AND CONSULTANT:
Erwin Pfeil and Fred Compton

German born and European trained, Erwin Pfeil has been in command of the kitchen at The Golden Lamb, Lebanon, Ohio, since 1969. During his tenure at Ohio's oldest inn, Chef Pfeil cooked for the first Reagan inaugural and was voted as having the "Best American Kitchen" by *Cincinnati Magazine*. Fred Compton is resident historian at The Golden Lamb. He began his career there as a busboy in 1966, working throughout high school and college. Mr. Compton has appeared on Home and Garden Television and C-Span, and his newspaper column, *Historically Speaking*, appears throughout southwestern Ohio.

Joaquín Sorolla y Bastida (Spanish, 1863–1923), *William Howard Taft,* **1909, oil on canvas, h. 59 x w. 31½ in. Bequest of Mr. and Mrs. Charles Phelps Taft**

*P*residing over the President's Room, William Howard Taft smiles jovially from his portrait by Joaquín Sorolla y Bastida. Charles and Anna Taft commissioned this portrait of the 27th President of the United States—and Charles's younger half-brother—at the White House in 1909, the year Taft took office. Before and after his term of office, Will, as he was called by his family, was a frequent visitor to the house on Pike Street, where he certainly would have enjoyed a meal such as this all-American menu.

A President in the Family

The house on Pike Street was like a second home to William Howard Taft (1857–1930). His future wife, Nellie Herron, lived across the street, certainly a potent draw during the years of their courtship. In 1883 he was also left to keep David Sinton company while Charles and Anna Taft took their family to vacation at Kennebunkport. "The young lawyer, now in partnership with Major Lloyd, wrote to his father that if any of Mr. Sinton's Presbyterian friends were to stand near the front door on a Sunday afternoon they would hear a sound remarkably like the click of billiard balls" (Ross, p. 79).

By far the most important connection of William Howard Taft to the house, however, is related to his candidacy for President of the United States. Charles devoted a year to the campaign, leading up to the Republican Convention in Chicago on June 16, 1908. When the ballots had been counted, Will won. From then on, Charles could enjoy the fruits of his efforts for it was "all Will everywhere—buttons, flags, pictures."

"The family gathered for the notification ceremonies, which were held in July at the Pike Street house in Cincinnati. The historic porch was decorated with garlands, banners, flags. The thunder of guns and bursting of bombs ushered in the day and the flag was run up in the old Taft garden. Yale and Woodward students wore their class colors. Fred Grant was there with survivors of the Civil War, and a fife and drum corps of gray-haired veterans. The large hats and flimsy muslins of the Edwardian era gave the lawn a garden party air. . . . The city was crowded with celebrants. Japanese lanterns with Taft banners were strung along the hillsides, and sirens and whistles kept up a din. At night there were fireworks in Eden Park, for Ohio was 'en fete.' Once again it was giving the nation a President" (Ross, pp. 197–99).

C. A. Davis, *Panoramic Photograph*
of William Howard Taft's Notification Day Ceremonies, **1908,**
published in the Cincinnati *Times-Star.*

Scalloped Oysters

½ cup dry white bread crumbs

1 cup cracker crumbs

½ cup melted butter

1 pint canned oysters

Salt and pepper

½ cup oyster liquor

2 tablespoons milk or cream

- Preheat oven to 400°. Mix bread and cracker crumbs and stir in butter. Press a thin layer of the crumb mixture (about one third) in the bottom of a greased 8-inch baking dish. Cover with half the drained oysters and sprinkle with salt and pepper. Combine the oyster liquor and milk or cream. Pour half the mixture over the oysters. Repeat, topping with the remaining crumbs. Bake 30 minutes.

Yield: 4 to 6 servings

Contributor: Patricia Charles, Taft Museum Docent

Because this is a rich dish, it may serve as many as 6 to 8 people when served as part of a large meal, such as Thanksgiving.

Mashed Potatoes and Turnips

8 white potatoes, peeled and cubed

Small amount of warm whole milk

3 tablespoons butter

Salt and pepper

3 or 4 turnips, peeled and cubed

- Cook potatoes in salted water until tender. Drain well. Add milk, butter, salt, and pepper, and mash until smooth.

- In a separate saucepan, cook turnips 20 to 30 minutes until tender. Drain well. Return to pan and shake over heat until completely dry. Mash. Add to mashed potatoes with enough warm milk to bring to desired texture.

Yield: 12 servings

The turnips must be as dry as you can get them, or this dish will be watery.

This dish is a delicious alternative to regular mashed potatoes.

Corn Pudding

6 tablespoons flour

3 teaspoons sugar

1½ teaspoons salt

3 cups whole kernel fresh or frozen
    corn, thawed

3 eggs, well beaten

1½ tablespoons butter, melted

3 cups milk

- Preheat oven to 350°. Combine flour, sugar, salt, and corn. Blend eggs, butter, and milk and add to corn mixture. Pour into a greased 2½- to 3-quart baking dish.
- Bake for 1 hour. Stir from bottom 2 or 3 times during first 30 minutes of baking time.

Yield: 6 servings

Well-drained canned corn may be substituted for the fresh or frozen corn.

Lemon-Glazed Carrots and Rutabagas

1 pound medium carrots

1 small rutabaga

½ cup water

2 tablespoons butter

2 tablespoons brown sugar

½ teaspoon grated lemon zest

2 tablespoons fresh lemon juice

¼ teaspoon salt

¼ teaspoon dried dill

- Julienne carrots and rutabaga into 3-inch strips. Combine vegetables and water in a saucepan. Bring to a boil, cover, reduce heat, and simmer 15 minutes. Remove from pan and drain well.
- Melt butter in saucepan. Stir in sugar, lemon zest and juice, salt, and dill until sugar dissolves. Return vegetables to pan, stirring often until vegetables are thoroughly heated.

Yield: 8 servings

Trifle

Custard

2 cups milk

6 egg yolks

½ cup sugar

¼ teaspoon salt

2 teaspoons vanilla

- Scald the milk in a large saucepan. Beat egg yolks and sugar until thick and light, about 3 to 4 minutes. Stir in the hot milk.

- Return mixture to pan and heat gently over low heat, stirring constantly with a wooden spoon. When the custard thickens slightly, about 10 minutes, remove it from the heat and continue stirring for 1 to 2 minutes. Custard is the correct consistency when you can draw your finger slowly across the wooden spoon and leave a clear trail. Do not overcook or boil the custard, or it will curdle. Cool.

Cake and Fruit

2 to 3 jelly rolls, sliced ½ inch thick

1 to 2 cups dry sherry

1 (16-ounce) can mixed fruit

1 (16-ounce) can diced pears

1 (16-ounce) can tangerines

1 cup heavy cream

Dark chocolate and cherries for garnish

- Dip one side of each slice of jelly roll into sherry and arrange in a bricklike fashion around the sides of a large deep clear glass bowl. Drain all the fruits well. Mix together and pour into the center of the bowl. Pour the cooled custard over the fruit and let stand for about 30 minutes.

- Whip the cream until soft peaks form. Spread over the trifle. Garnish with shaved dark chocolate and cherries.

Yield: 16 servings

Contributor: Richard King, Richard's Hair Salon, Hyde Park

While not difficult, this recipe requires 2 to 2½ hours to prepare. You will, however, win raves from your guests to compensate for the time you spend.

A traditional English dessert, trifle immigrated to the fledgling United States with many other dishes. It is light enough to serve after even a large rich meal.

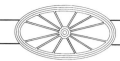

Apple Crisp

4 cups sliced cooking apples

1 teaspoon cinnamon

1 teaspoon salt

¼ cup water

¾ cup sifted flour

1 cup sugar

⅓ cup butter

Ice cream or sharp cheddar cheese

- Preheat oven to 350°. Butter a 10 by 6 by 2 inch baking dish. Arrange apples in the dish. Sprinkle with cinnamon, salt, and water.

- Cut flour and sugar into butter. Drop mixture over apples. Bake 40 minutes. Serve warm with ice cream or cheese.

Yield: 6 servings

Contributor: Jane Young, Taft Museum Docent

A Taste of Italy

— *Malta Gray Room* —

A Taste of Italy
— Malta Gray Room —

Menu

Antipasti
Scampi e Carciofini alla Bungustaio
(Scampi and Artichokes Appetizer)

Minestre
Minestra di Piselli con Uova
(Peas and Eggs Soup)

Pasta
Pasta con Broccoli e Fungi Provençal
(Pasta with Broccoli and Mushrooms)

Insalata
Insalata Cipolle Cotte di Pomodori
(Cooked Onion and Fresh Tomato Salad)

Rollatini (Veal, Pork, or Chicken) with Marsala, Provençal, or Creamy Gorgonzola Sauce

Dolce
Biscuit Tortoni

MENU CHAIRWOMAN:
Ruth Lowenthal, Taft Museum Docent

CHEFS:
Odessa and Salvatore Barresi

When the Barresi family enterprise began in Cincinnati with six tables, there was no menu. Each customer wanted a special dish and would not settle for less. Fortunately, neither would Sal. Because Sal's father, Pietro, came from Genoa in northern Italy and his mother, Amalia, hailed from the southern olive oil region near Calabria, Sal's dishes reflect the best of both cuisines. Today, Baressi's boasts 28 tables in elegant dining rooms and an extensive menu, with each dish still personally prepared by Sal and Odessa.

Master of the Taft Orpheus, *Display Dish with Orpheus Lamenting the Death of Eurydice,* **Faenza, about 1520–30, maiolica, diam. 16¼ in. Bequest of Mr. and Mrs. Charles Phelps Taft**

The Italian maiolica plates, dishes, and ewers (early 16th century) on display in the Malta Gray Room, accompanied by Renaissance treasures from France as well, evoke a sunny clime. While most of the maiolica dishes were made for display, not for everyday use, some of the plates would have been used to present gifts of sweets—perhaps such as the Biscuit Tortoni recipe found here—to a lover. The delicious and timeless food of Italy, cradle of the Renaissance, bears out the richness and beauty of its art.

Renaissance Man

Before he became President of the United States (1909–13) and later chief justice of the Supreme Court (1921–30)—the only person in American history to hold both posts—William Howard Taft served as civil governor of the Philippines, where he and his wife, Nellie, lived from 1901 to 1904. During his tenure, he subordinated military to civil command, instituted land reform, sponsored a road-construction program, and, in general, prepared the Filipino people for self-government.

In 1904 when "the Tafts, as a friendly gesture of departure, gave a huge Venetian masked ball and carnival, considerable difficulty was encountered in deciding upon a suitable Venetian character for the Governor to represent, since his physique did not readily lend itself to disguise. He wrote to his brother Charles:

" 'It is a humiliating fact to me that every suggestion of a character for me has been summarily rejected by Nellie unless it involved wearing a gown of such voluminous proportions as to conceal my Apollo-like form completely. The proposal that I assume the character of an Igarrote chieftain because of the slight drain on capital and our costuming resources did not meet with favor. So it is settled that I must assume the robes and headgear of the husband of the Adriatic, the Doge of Venice. The question is whether the robe can be made historically accurate and at the same time so conceal my nether extremities as to make it unnecessary for me to dye my nether undergarments to a proper color, for the entire Orient cannot produce tights of a sufficient size. The Council of War, meaning Nellie, has not advised me on the subject, but tights or no tights we shall have a Doge of Venice that was never on land or sea' " (Duffy, p. 165).

Charles Phelps Taft (left) and William Howard Taft in front of the Pike Street house in April 1908. Photograph courtesy of the National Park Service

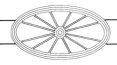
Scampi e Carciofini alla Bungustaio
(Scampi and Artichokes Appetizer)

1 pound small raw shrimp in shell

1 (15-ounce) can artichoke hearts

¼ cup olive oil

1 small onion, diced

2 cloves garlic, chopped

1 tablespoon chopped fresh basil

Juice of half a lemon

Salt and pepper

Grated fresh Parmesan cheese

- Boil shrimp in a little water for about 5 minutes (or sauté briefly in a little olive oil) until just done. Shell, devein, and set aside. Drain artichokes, cut into quarters, and set aside.

- Heat olive oil in a sauté pan over medium heat. Sauté onion for about 1 minute. Add garlic and sauté another minute. Add shrimp and continue to sauté for 3 minutes longer. Add artichokes and basil and sauté for 2 additional minutes. Add lemon juice, salt, and pepper; stir gently.

- Serve hot or cold as an appetizer. Pass cheese when serving.

Yield: 6 servings

Serve this appetizer over pasta as a delicious Italian main dish.

Minestra di Piselli con Uova
(Peas and Eggs Soup)

1 cup chicken broth

2 cups water

½ pound fresh or frozen peas, thawed

3 tablespoons olive oil

1 small onion, chopped

¼ cup peeled, diced fresh tomato

½ teaspoon dried oregano

2 large eggs, lightly beaten

1 tablespoon chopped fresh parsley

2 tablespoons grated fresh Parmesan
    or Romano cheese

Salt and pepper

- Bring broth and water to a boil in soup pot. Add fresh peas and cook briefly until peas are almost tender. (Do not add frozen peas at this time.)

- Meanwhile heat olive oil in a skillet over medium heat. Add onion and sauté for 1 minute. Add tomato and oregano and simmer for 5 minutes. Add to boiling broth and continue simmering for 10 minutes.

- Combine eggs, parsley, and cheese and mix well. (Add frozen peas to broth at this time.) Slowly drizzle egg mixture into broth while stirring gently and continuously. Simmer for 2 minutes. Season with salt and pepper.

- Serve hot with additional cheese on the side.

Yield: 8 servings

This flavorful, light soup is perfect for serving before a rich entrée.

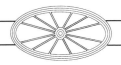

Pasta con Broccoli e Fungi Provençal

(Pasta with Broccoli and Mushrooms)

¼ cup olive oil

1 tablespoon butter

3 cloves garlic chopped

1 bunch scallions

1½ cups sliced mushrooms (various kinds)

1 cup peeled, diced fresh tomato

1½ cups small broccoli florets

½ cup chicken broth

¼ cup heavy cream

¼ cup grated fresh Parmesan or Romano cheese

Salt and pepper

½ pound angel hair pasta (fresh or dried)

- Heat olive oil and butter carefully in a large skillet so as not to burn the butter. Add garlic and scallions and sauté for 2 minutes. Add mushrooms and continue to sauté 4 minutes longer.

- One at time, stirring gently all the while, add tomato, broccoli, chicken broth, cream, and cheese. Cover and simmer for about 3 minutes. Uncover, remove from heat, and season with salt and pepper.

- Meanwhile, cook fresh pasta for 2 minutes in boiling water with a pinch of salt or prepare dried pasta according to package directions. Toss drained pasta with sauce.

- Serve hot with more cheese on the side.

Yield: 4 to 6 side dish servings

For a lower fat version of this dish, you may omit the butter, cream, and cheese and increase the chicken broth to 1 cup. For a main dish, add cooked chicken or shrimp.

Insalata Cipolle Cotte di Pomodori
(Cooked Onion and Fresh Tomato Salad)

3 medium onions

3 tablespoons olive oil

5 large ripe tomatoes

⅓ cup olive oil

⅓ cup balsamic vinegar

10 fresh basil leaves, coarsely chopped

1 teaspoon oregano

Salt and pepper

- Peel onions and slice and divide into circles. Heat olive oil in a skillet and sauté onions until wilted. Set aside.

- Slice tomatoes into circles and arrange the large center slices on 8 salad plates. Top tomatoes with a small amount of cooked onion. Drizzle each salad with olive oil and vinegar. Sprinkle with basil, oregano, salt, and freshly ground pepper.

Yield: 8 servings

Add slices of fresh mozzarella and grilled eggplant to make a light summer lunch served with crusty bread and fresh fruit.

This salad is perfect with fresh garden tomatoes and basil. In the winter, Roma tomatoes, while smaller and changing the appearance of the dish, often have a better flavor and texture than the other tomatoes available at many supermarkets.

Rollatini (Veal, Pork, or Chicken) with Marsala, Provençal, or Creamy Gorgonzola Sauce

Rollatini

1½ pounds fresh spinach leaves

4 tablespoons grated fresh Parmesan cheese

1 egg

1½ pounds thinly sliced veal, pork tenderloin, or chicken breast

⅓ pound prosciutto (or thinly sliced cooked ham)

¼ teaspoon sage

3 tablespoons olive oil

1 tablespoon butter

2 cloves garlic, cut in half

- Preheat oven to 325°. Wash and drain (but do not dry) the spinach. Place in a large skillet over moderate heat just to wilt, about 5 minutes. Let cool in a colander, then squeeze dry and chop finely. In a large bowl, combine spinach, cheese, and egg. Mix well.

- Pound the slices of meat until thin between sheets of waxed paper. Place each slice of meat on a sheet of waxed paper or plastic wrap. Spread each slice with spinach mixture, layer with prosciutto slices, and sprinkle with sage. Using the waxed paper or plastic wrap, roll each slice tightly, like a jelly roll. Tie with kitchen string or secure with meat skewers.

- In a large skillet, heat olive oil, butter, and garlic over medium heat. Add meat rolls and brown on all sides. Place browned rolls in a roasting pan, cover, and bake for 30 minutes. Serve with Marsala, Provençal, or Creamy Gorgonzola Sauce.

Marsala Sauce

2 tablespoons butter

2 tablespoons flour

½ cup dry Marsala

2½ cups veal stock (or chicken or beef broth)

1 cup sliced mushrooms

¼ cup pine nuts

Salt and pepper

- In a saucepan, heat butter over medium heat. As soon as the butter melts, whisk in the flour. Add Marsala and cook for 2 minutes. Add stock and reduce by boiling for 5 minutes. Add mushrooms and pine nuts. Simmer 5 minutes longer. Season with salt and pepper.

Rollatini continued on next page

Rollatini continued

Provençal Sauce

3 tablespoons olive oil

1 tablespoon butter

1 small onion, diced

3 cloves garlic, chopped

1 cup diced fresh tomato

½ cup chicken stock

¼ cup chopped scallions

Salt and pepper

1 tablespoon chopped fresh parsley

1 tablespoon chopped fresh basil

¼ cup grated fresh Romano or Parmesan cheese

- In a medium skillet, heat olive oil and butter over medium heat and sauté onion and garlic for 2 minutes. Add tomatoes and chicken stock and simmer for 3 to 4 minutes. Add scallions, salt, and pepper and simmer 1 minute longer. Remove from heat and stir in parsley, basil, and cheese.

Creamy Gorgonzola Sauce

1 cup heavy cream

2 tablespoons butter

2 tablespoons flour

½ cup sliced mushrooms

½ cup Gorgonzola cheese

¼ teaspoon ground nutmeg

Salt and pepper

- Warm cream in a small saucepan. In a medium skillet, melt butter over medium heat. Whisk in flour. Add warmed cream, whisking rapidly until well blended and slightly thickened. Lower heat, add mushrooms, and cook for 3 to 4 minutes. Add Gorgonzola, nutmeg, salt, and pepper. Stir until creamy.

Yield: 6 to 8 servings

The rollatini may be prepared ahead of time and reheated just before serving.

Any of the sauces may also be served over your choice of pasta for a tasty side dish.

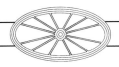
Biscuit Tortoni

½ cup sliced almonds, crushed

2 cups heavy cream

⅓ cup powdered sugar

11 tablespoons Amaretto, divided use

½ cup crushed almond cookies

Fresh fruit or berries

- In a dry medium skillet, toast crushed almonds. Set aside to cool.
- In a medium bowl, whip cream until soft peaks form. Add sugar and whip until firm but not dry. Quickly whip in 3 tablespoons of Amaretto. Gently fold in almonds and cookies. Spoon mixture into paper or foil cup–lined muffin tins and freeze for about 2 hours.
- Remove paper or foil cups. Serve each inverted on a plate surrounded by fresh fruit or berries and topped with 1 tablespoon of Amaretto.

Alternate Preparation: Crust

½ cup sliced almonds, crushed and toasted

½ cup crushed almond cookies

3 tablespoons butter, melted

- Combine all crust ingredients and press into the bottom of an 8-inch springform pan. Top with the recipe for Biscuit Tortoni above and freeze. Allow to thaw slightly before cutting, serving, and garnishing as above.

Yield: 8 servings

Substitute any dessert liqueur for the Amaretto for a different flavor.

This rich dessert is nicely complemented by a cup of espresso.

Afternoon Tea with the Ladies

— *Gray Room* —

Afternoon Tea with the Ladies
— *Gray Room* —

Menu

Mushroom Tea Points

Deviled Ham Toasts

Tangy Egg Salad Sandwiches

Chilled Cucumber Fingers

Currant Cakes

Raspberry Raisin Scone Cake

Rock Cakes

MENU CHAIRWOMAN:
Eileen Harsnett, Taft Museum Docent

For this menu, Eileen Harsnett found her inspiration in *The London Ritz Book of Afternoon Tea: The Art and Pleasures of Taking Tea* by Helen Simpson (London, 1986), adding American variations to the recipes. You and your guests (ladies and gentlemen alike) will savor these delicious sandwiches and sweets with steaming Earl Gray or Darjeeling tea served in your best china teacups.

Gray Room of the Taft Museum

*B*ehind the bland and aristocratic faces of the ladies portrayed by Thomas Gainsborough, Sir Joshua Reynolds, and Henry Raeburn in this former parlor of the Taft home lies many a tale. The lady over the fireplace, for example, depicted in a thoughtful pose by Gainsborough, is Maria Walpole, illegitimate daughter of Sir Edward Walpole. After the death of her first husband, she eloped with the duke of Gloucester, brother to the king of England, so angering the royal family that they forced the Royal Marriage Bill through Parliament in 1772 to prevent further unions of royalty to illegitimate offspring. Now that's a story as tasty as the tea sandwiches, cakes, and cookies in this 20th-century tea menu.

If These Walls Could Talk

Like finger sandwiches and tea scones, the following excerpts offer up small bites of some of the many people, from visiting dignitaries to local philanthropists, who were guests of the famous hosts of Pike Street.

"For more than a century socialite Cincinnatians and many artists, writers, and musicians came here to attend receptions, dinners, musicales, and balls. Often the guest of honor was a notable. At one time or another Robert Owen; Frances Trollope; Bernhard, Duke of Saxe-Weimar; William Henry Harrison; Albert, King of the Belgians; and Cardinal Mercier were guests" (WPA, p. 166).

"In the early 1850s Annie Rivers Longworth was entertaining her guests at one of her famous weekly 'teas under the hackberry,' a huge tree which grew on the front lawn" (Boehle, p. 20).

"It is fitting that we place on record the visit, on October 22, 1919, of their Majesties the King and Queen of the Belgians, to the home of Mr. and Mrs. Taft. For on that day Cincinnati devoted itself whole-heartedly to the solemnity of so rare an occasion" (Brockwell, p. xiv).

On the death of Charles Phelps Taft in 1929, it was noted, "For half a century artists, writers, musicians, world statesmen, jurists and diplomats, royalty and struggling poets had dined at his board. William H. Taft had made his acceptance speech from his porch, and other high points of his career were associated with the Pike Street house" (Ross, p. 360).

The Cincinnati *Times-Star* of November 30, 1932, noted the following regarding the grand opening festivities for the Taft Museum: "Mrs. George H. Warrington, Mrs. John J. Rowe, Mrs. Robert A. Taft and Mrs. Russell Wilson were in charge of the floral decorations and the buffet supper served by the Queen City Club—massive silver bowls of white chrysanthemums, white roses and calla lilies and heavy silver candelabra decorated the supper table which was arranged in the lecture hall."

If these walls could talk, they could share many a story of the goings on over teacups and punch bowls, around dinner tables and in reception lines. For, between 1820 and 1931—and continuing today—both visitors to Cincinnati and local folks stop to enjoy the hospitality of the house on Pike Street.

**Anna Sinton Taft escorts
King Albert I and Queen Elizabeth of Belgium
(to her left and right) up the front walk to the
Pike Street house on October 22, 1919.
Collection of Cincinnati Museum Center, no. A-81-174**

Mushroom Tea Points

3 large mushrooms

Juice of one lemon

Butter, softened, divided use

1 egg, beaten

Salt, pepper, and cayenne pepper

1 teaspoon grated fresh Parmesan cheese

2 thin slices white bread

- Poach the mushrooms in the lemon juice and 1 teaspoon butter for about 8 minutes. Meanwhile, lightly scramble the egg in a little butter.

- Remove mushrooms from heat, drain and discard the poaching liquid, and lightly mash to form a paste. Season with salt, pepper, and cayenne. Add softened butter, about equal to the amount of mushroom paste. Stir in the scrambled egg and Parmesan cheese.

- Spread mushroom mixture on the slices of bread. Remove the crusts and cut into triangles.

Yield: 8 small sandwiches

Serve cold on a platter garnished with sprigs of parsley and wedges of hard cooked egg lightly sprinkled with curry powder.

Deviled Ham Toasts

4 thin slices white bread, toasted

⅓ cup chopped lean ham

2 teaspoons Worcestershire sauce

Cayenne pepper

2 teaspoons French mustard

1 tablespoon butter

1 tablespoon chopped fresh parsley

- Cut 4 circles from each slice of toast with a 2-inch cutter or a sharp knife using a small glass for a template.

- Combine the ham, Worcestershire sauce, cayenne, and mustard. Melt the butter in a small skillet. Add the ham mixture and heat until sizzling. Pile ham mixture onto toast rounds, sprinkle with parsley, and serve hot.

Yield: 16 tea sandwiches

These tangy sandwiches are best on very thin slices of toast; use a rolling pin to flatten slices of bread slightly before toasting.

The toast rounds and ham mixture may be prepared in advance to heat and assemble just before serving.

Tangy Egg Salad Sandwiches

½ small onion

1 egg, hard cooked and chopped

1 tablespoon mayonnaise

Pinch English dry mustard

2 or 3 drops each lemon juice and
   Worcestershire sauce

Butter, softened

2 thin slices white or whole wheat
   bread

8 pimiento slices

- Scrape the cut side of the onion over a small bowl to extract ½ teaspoon of juicy purée. Combine onion purée, egg, mayonnaise, mustard, lemon juice, and Worcestershire sauce.

- Butter the bread. Spread egg mixture on one slice of bread and top with second slice. Pound or roll the sandwich lightly to make very thin. Remove crusts, and cut into four squares or triangles. Garnish each sandwich with two crossed pimiento slices.

Yield: 4 tea sandwiches

Chilled Cucumber Fingers

1 medium cucumber

Sprinkle of vinegar and salt

8 thin slices soft whole wheat bread

- Peel the cucumber and cut into transparent slices with the slicing side of a grater, mandolin, or potato peeler. Sprinkle with a little vinegar and salt. Let sit for half an hour. Drain the cucumbers well by shuffling the slices in a sieve or strainer.

- Cover 4 slices of bread with 2 layers of cucumber slices. Top with remaining bread. Press each sandwich firmly but delicately with the palm of your hand. Remove crusts and cut each sandwich into 3 rectangles. Place on a glass or glazed ceramic serving plate and cover with a lightly dampened tea towel. Refrigerate. Serve very cold.

Yield: 12 finger sandwiches

These simple fingers are moist and refreshing.

Currant Cakes

1 cup currants

1 sheet puff pastry, thawed

½ cup sugar

Milk and sugar for glazing

- Pour boiling water to cover over the currants. Let stand until the currants are plump.

- Preheat oven to 375°. Grease a baking sheet. Roll out puff pastry until it is about 12 inches square. Use a large glass or biscuit cutter to cut out 4-inch rounds. Drain currants and stir in sugar.

- Place a small spoonful of currant mixture into the center of each pastry round. Dampen the edges of the pastry with water, and gather edges together around the currants to form a small bundle. Turn the bundles over and press with a rolling pin until they are 4-inch rounds again. The shadow of the currants will show through the pastry.

- Brush each cake with milk and sprinkle lightly with sugar. Use the tip of a knife to make three parallel slits through the top of the pastry, just to reveal the currants. Bake on the center rack of the oven for 15 to 20 minutes until golden. Serve warm or at room temperature.

Yield: 9 cakes

In England, these rich, fruity cakes are traditionally called Eccles cakes, after a town in Lancashire. The three slits on the top are said to represent the Holy Trinity.

Raspberry Raisin Scone Cake

2 cups all-purpose flour

2 tablespoons sugar

1 tablespoon baking powder

¼ teaspoon salt

½ cup butter

½ cup whole milk

2 eggs, beaten

¾ cup raisins

½ cup raspberry jam

Melted butter and powdered sugar

- Have all ingredients at room temperature. Preheat oven to 425°.

- Combine flour, sugar, baking powder, and salt. Cut in the butter to a crumb-like texture. Mix in milk, eggs, and raisins until the dough is firm and smooth.

- Pat half the dough into the bottom of a greased 8-inch round cake pan, extending it up the sides to form a rim about ¼ inch high. Spread jam evenly over the dough. Stretch and pat the remaining dough smoothly over the top to cover the jam.

- Use a sharp knife to score the top into 8 wedges. Brush with melted butter and sprinkle with powdered sugar. Bake for 20 to 25 minutes, or until a toothpick inserted in the center comes out clean.

Yield: 8 servings

Bring this rich cake to the tea table whole on a cake plate. To serve each guest, cut wedges along the scored lines.

Rock Cakes

1½ **cups self-rising flour**

Pinch of salt

4 tablespoons butter

¼ **cup shortening**

½ **cup sugar**

⅔ **cup currants**

1 egg

1 tablespoon milk

- Preheat oven to 400°. Combine flour and salt. Cut in the butter and shortening to a crumb-like texture. Use a knife to stir in the sugar and currants until the dough is well mixed and speckled. Beat the egg with the milk and add to the flour mixture, stirring with a fork until it is stiff.

- Drop tablespoons of dough onto greased baking sheets. Bake 15 to 20 minutes until lightly browned. Cool on a wire rack.

Yield: 12 cookies

For a sweeter confection, use a little glaze to ice Rock Cakes.

Ideal for snacks, tea time, or picnics, these little cakes have a rough and craggy appearance but are short and sweet to taste.

A Mediterranean Feast

— Violet and Gray Room —

A Mediterranean Feast
— Violet and Gray Room —

Menu

Appetizer
Baked Stuffed Brie in Puff Pastry

Soup
Venetian Minestrone

Salad
Sicilian Tomato Salad

Entrée
Chef Anna Gherardi's Salmon with Mustard-Tarragon Champagne Sauce
Asparagus with Papaya Relish
Herb Biscuits

Dessert
"Spiced" Caramel Flan

MENU CHAIRWOMAN:
Vivian Adams-Dobur, Taft Museum Docent

CHEF:
Jimmy Gherardi

When not occupied with his roles as radio host, television personality, and teacher, Jimmy Gherardi is entertaining someone in one of his restaurants or taking part in charity events. Chef Gherardi's greatest satisfaction is educating people about food and wine. He shares his knowledge at seminars, college classrooms, and culinary schools. J's, his seafood restaurant in Cincinnati, has been recognized for excellence locally and nationally and was selected by *Wine Enthusiast* as one of the top 27 U.S. restaurants for food and wine.

J. M. W. Turner (English, 1775–1851), *Europa and the Bull*,
about 1840–50, oil on canvas, h. 35⅞ x w. 47⅞ in.
Bequest of Mr. and Mrs. Charles Phelps Taft

The myth of Europa and the Bull, depicted with golden sands and azure sea by James Mallord William Turner, inspired this Mediterranean menu. One of Turner's last great paintings, *Europa and the Bull* focuses on the dramatic moment when Zeus, disguised as a white bull, carries the princess Europa into the sea, bound for Crete, while her companions gesture helplessly on the shore. According to legend, Europa and Zeus have three children, including King Minos, and the bull becomes the constellation Taurus.

Old Nick and Honest Abe

On a summer day, in 1857, a tall man who appeared to have outgrown his clothes, hesitatingly passed through the Pike Street gate. . . .

In the middle of the gravel path leading to a pillared portico, a small, queerly dressed old man with no appearance whatever of having outgrown his old-fashioned raiment was weeding. Loose pantaloons lay in folds over "Old Nick's" latchets, and a shirt with a huge collar almost obscured his ears.

"Excuse me, but I have heard a good deal about the beauty of these grounds, and would be interested in seeing them. Does your master allow visitors to his premises?"

The seeming gardener rose to his feet and as was his wont, began a slow survey of his tall interlocutor. Such demands were not infrequent, but the person before him appeared unusual and perhaps would not say stereotyped things. Commencing at the stranger's feet, Longworth's glance traveled methodically up the spare, gaunt limbs to the long coat which hung—but not in "ample folds"—from angular shoulders, then rested some minutes on the plain, almost harsh face with its keen, kindly, gray eyes.

"My master is a queer duck. He doesn't allow strangers to come in, but he makes an exception every time one does come. He would be glad in this case to consider you a friend, sir. But before viewing the garden, perhaps you would like to taste his wine."

"Excuse me, Mr. Longworth, mine was a foolish mistake!"

"Not at all. I am quite used to it; in fact, you are the first to find me out so soon. That's my loss, perhaps. Sometimes I get ten cents and sometimes as much as a quarter for showing visitors my gardens. In fact, I might say it's the only honest money I ever made, having been, by profession, a lawyer!"

"So am I!"

Longworth's quizzical smile broadened. "Well, if you are of the fraternity, there is no reason why two fellow scamps should not shake hands! Are you here on business?"

"I came with that understanding. Unfortunately, however, I seem to have lost the job. I was retained to defend a patent-reaper suit against one of the big men from Baltimore, Reveredy Johnson. I confess it had been my ambition to measure swords with him, the best at the bar from common report."

"Well, why don't you, having been retained?"

"Most likely the defense got scared and opined that Abraham Lincoln was no match for a celebrity" (Chambrun, *Longworth*, pp. 36–38).

Nicholas Longworth at His Desk, **daguerreotype**

82

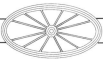
Baked Stuffed Brie in Puff Pastry

Puff Pastry

6 cups flour

10 tablespoons butter

1 tablespoon salt

⅔ cup water

Filling

1 pound fresh spinach

1 tomato, chopped

3 cloves garlic, chopped

1 tablespoon butter

Salt and pepper

**1 small French Brie cheese round
(5-inch diameter)**

- Place the flour in the large bowl of an electric mixer. In a small saucepan, combine butter, salt, and water, and bring to a boil. Pour the boiling butter mixture into the flour and mix until the dough is well blended and forms a ball. Wrap in a damp cloth and chill for 1 to 2 hours.

- Wash and dry the spinach. Sauté spinach, tomato, and garlic in butter. Season with salt and pepper and let cool.

- Preheat the oven to 375°. Cut the Brie in half horizontally. Spread the bottom half with the spinach mixture and top with the remaining half.

- Roll the puff pastry and cut out two circles each about 8 inches in diameter. Brush the edges of the pastry with water. Place the filled Brie on one pastry circle and top with the other pastry circle. Gently pinch the edges together to close. Place on a baking sheet and bake for 10 to 15 minutes. Allow to cool before cutting into wedges to serve.

Yield: 8 servings

Substitute frozen, prepared puff pastry to save time and effort.

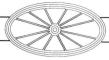

Venetian Minestrone

2 tablespoons unsalted butter

4 tablespoons olive oil

2 large onions, chopped

3 to 4 cloves garlic, minced

4 medium zucchini, diced

2 celery ribs, chopped

2 medium potatoes, diced

2 medium carrots, peeled and diced

1 (1-pound) head green cabbage, cored and chopped

1 bay leaf

2 tablespoons fresh sage, chopped

4 quarts water

Salt and pepper

Grated fresh Romano cheese

- In a large soup pot, heat the butter and olive oil over medium heat. Add the onions and garlic and sauté until transparent, about 10 minutes. Add the remaining vegetables, bay leaf, and sage and continue cooking for about 15 to 20 minutes, stirring frequently.

- Add water and bring to a boil. Reduce heat and simmer 15 to 20 minutes until carrots and potatoes are cooked. Season with salt and pepper. Remove and discard bay leaf. Serve with grated Romano cheese on the side.

Yield: 8 servings

This hearty, satisfying soup may be prepared one day in advance and reheated to serve.

Sicilian Tomato Salad

½ cup olive oil

2 tablespoons red wine vinegar

2 cloves garlic, chopped

1 small red onion, halved and thinly sliced

½ teaspoon sugar

½ teaspoon dried oregano

4 to 6 fresh basil leaves, torn into pieces

Salt and pepper

3 to 4 ripe tomatoes, cut into wedges

Romaine lettuce leaves

This colorful salad is both tasty and timeless.

- Combine all ingredients, except tomatoes and lettuce, and mix well. Add tomatoes and toss gently but thoroughly to combine. Marinate at room temperature for about 1 hour.

- Serve on romaine lettuce leaves.

Yield: 8 servings

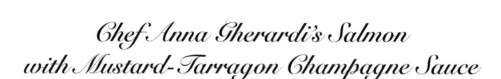
Chef Anna Gherardi's Salmon with Mustard-Tarragon Champagne Sauce

8 salmon fillets, about 6 ounces each

1 bottle champagne or sparkling wine

3 cups heavy cream

Salt and white pepper

3 tablespoons prepared Dijon mustard

2 tablespoons fresh tarragon, snipped

Sprigs of fresh tarragon for garnish

- Place salmon fillets in a pan large enough to hold them in one layer. Add 2 cups water and half the bottle of champagne. Bring to a simmer and poach over low heat for 10 to 12 minutes or until the salmon is fully cooked. Remove from heat.

- In a saucepan, bring cream, salt, and pepper to a boil. Whisk in mustard and remaining champagne. Reduce heat and simmer until the sauce thickens somewhat. Stir in tarragon. Keep warm.

- Remove salmon from poaching liquid and blot dry. To serve, divide sauce among 8 dinner plates. Place one fillet on top of sauce on each plate. Garnish with a sprig of tarragon.

Yield: 8 servings

This elegant entrée is delicate in flavor and easy to make.

Asparagus with Papaya Relish

48 asparagus spears

1 yellow bell pepper

1 papaya

1 tomato

¼ cup rice vinegar

½ cup salad oil

Salt and white pepper

2 tablespoons chopped pickled ginger

2 teaspoons chopped garlic

2 tablespoons toasted or black sesame
    seeds

- Trim tough ends from the asparagus and cook in boiling water until tender-crisp. Immerse immediately in ice water to stop cooking. Clean, seed, and julienne the bell pepper. Chop the papaya in medium dice. Peel and chop the tomato in medium dice. Combine.

- Whisk together vinegar, oil, salt, pepper, ginger, and garlic. Pour over asparagus mixture. Marinate 2 to 4 hours.

- Serve on side of plate with Chef Anna Gherardi's Salmon with Mustard-Tarragon Champagne Sauce. Garnish with sesame seeds.

Yield: 8 servings

This relish may be prepared one day in advance.

Herb Biscuits

1¼ cups cake flour

¾ cup bread flour, plus ½ cup for kneading

1 teaspoon salt

1 tablespoon sugar

1 tablespoon baking powder

8 tablespoons butter, cubed

4 tablespoons finely chopped mixed fresh herbs (rosemary, basil, parsley)

2 eggs, divided use

6 tablespoons milk

6 tablespoons buttermilk

1 tablespoon water

- Sift dry ingredients together into a bowl. Knead butter into the mixture with your fingers until it reaches the consistency of coarse meal. Stir in herbs.

- In a small bowl, beat 1 egg with milk and buttermilk. Add to flour mixture and mix quickly just until combined. Flour a work surface and knead dough lightly. Refrigerate dough for 30 minutes.

- Preheat oven to 375°. Beat remaining egg with water. Set aside. Roll dough to a thickness of ½ inch on a floured work surface. Brush excess flour from dough. Cut out biscuits using a 1½-inch cutter or glass. Place on a parchment-lined baking sheet. Brush biscuit tops with egg wash.

- Bake for 15 minutes or until tops turn golden. Serve within 3 hours.

Yield: 24 biscuits

"Spiced" Caramel Flan

1½ cups milk

1½ cups heavy cream

1½ tablespoons pumpkin pie spice,
 plus a pinch, divided use

½ teaspoon ground allspice

3 whole vanilla beans, split lengthwise

6 egg yolks

3 eggs

1¼ cups sugar, plus 2 tablespoons,
 divided use

4 tablespoons water

2 drops lemon juice

Butter to grease ramekins

Fresh raspberries or strawberries

- In a 2-quart saucepan, combine milk, cream, 1½ tablespoons pumpkin pie spice, and allspice. Scrape the seeds from the vanilla beans and add along with the pods to the milk mixture. Bring to a boil over moderate heat. Remove from heat and set aside to cool.

- Place the egg yolks, eggs, and ½ cup sugar in a mixing bowl and whisk until light and creamy. Stir in the cooled milk and strain custard mixture.

- Preheat oven to 300°. Butter 8 small ramekins.

- In a small saucepan, combine the remaining sugar, pinch of pumpkin pie spice, water, and lemon juice. Bring to a boil over medium high heat, stirring occasionally with a wooden spoon until the sugar dissolves. Continue boiling without stirring, watching carefully until the caramel turns golden. Immediately pour hot caramel into the prepared ramekins to a depth of ¼ inch. When the caramel hardens, fill each ramekin with ½ cup custard.

- Lay a sheet of parchment paper in a deep roasting pan and place the ramekins on top. Fill the pan with hot water to a level halfway up the sides of the ramekins. Bake for 30 to 40 minutes until the custard is set. (Note: the water in the pan must not come to a boil or the custard will curdle.) Remove the ramekins from the water and set aside. When cool, cover with plastic wrap and refrigerate overnight.

- To serve, run a thin paring knife around the edge of the ramekin. Invert onto a small plate and gently remove the ramekin. Allow to warm to room temperature before serving garnished with fresh raspberries or strawberries.

Yield: 8 servings

This smooth, richly decadent dessert is a treat in any season.

Dutch Treat

— *Yellow Room* —

Dutch Treat
— Yellow Room —

Menu

Gersokte Zalm Salade met Bieslook Saus
(Smoked Salmon Salad with Chive Sauce)

Duivekater
(Holiday Sweet Bread)

Aardappelpannekoekjes
(Potato Pancakes)

Saus van Wintergroente
(Winter Vegetable Sauce)

Kaneel Stoofpeertjes
(Cinnamon Stewed Pears)

Citroentaart met Aardbeien
(Lemon Tart with Strawberries)

MENU CHAIRWOMAN:
Laura Fidler, Taft Museum Docent

Some of the recipes in this Dutch Treat are derived from *The Flavor of Holland* by Hilary Keatings and Anneke Peters (Haarlem, 1995). Modified and combined with recipes from Laura Fidler's friends and family, they make a fine and unusual alternative for an elegant luncheon or supper.

Pieter de Hooch (Dutch, 1629–1684),
A Woman with a Cittern and a Singing Couple at a Table,
about 1667, oil on canvas, h. 27⅞ x w. 22¾ in.
Bequest of Mr. and Mrs. Charles Phelps Taft

In the Yellow Room scenes of everyday life in 17th-century Holland depict both rich and poor, city and country. During this Golden Age of Dutch art, painters provided a ready market with images of peasant life, kitchen dramas, low-lying landscapes, local city scenes, and society gatherings. Scenes such as this musical party in an elegant interior by Pieter de Hooch attest to his reputation as Holland's quintessential painter of domestic life and provide inspiration for the refined fare of this Dutch Treat.

A Masterpiece and a Museum

In 1909 while on a cross-country tour President William Howard Taft visited his brother and sister-in-law in Cincinnati. "He found Charles and Annie rejoicing in the possession of another Rembrandt. It was so costly that Charles had said he would not buy it, but when [Henry C.] Frick threatened to get it unless Charles did, Annie felt that this was a challenge to a Sinton. It was exhibited later that year in New York when Scott & Fowles gave an exhibition of Taft paintings, including two by Frans Hals. 'I think they made quite a sensation in the New York art world,' Charles reported to Will. 'Our Rembrandt was also a ten-strike.' "

Years later "the meeting of the American Bar Association was held in Cincinnati . . . and many of the visiting jurists were entertained at the Pike Street house. Sir John Simon, over from England, was particularly impressed with the family paintings. He had the interest of an expert. . . . With William Howard Taft present they all discussed the great collection of pictures which Frick had given to New York, and his Fifth Avenue house that would be turned into a museum. Will speculated on what Charles and Annie might do with their collection. In course of time they did the same as Frick" (Ross, pp. 230, 326–27).

The Taft Residence in Cincinnati, **from** *The Museum News,*
**vol. VIII, no. 18 (Mar. 15, 1931), announcing the conversion of
the Taft house and collection to the Taft Museum**

Gerookte Zalm Salade met Bieslook Saus
(Smoked Salmon Salad with Chive Sauce)

4 fillets smoked salmon

1 teaspoon anise flavored liqueur

1 large cucumber

2 large tomatoes

½ tart apple

1 scallion

Salt and freshly ground black pepper

1 cup unsalted fish stock

1 small bunch chives

½ cup crème fraîche

- Cut each salmon fillet into 4 long strips, then across into small pieces. Place in a large bowl with the liqueur.

- Cut the cucumber in half, reserving half for garnish; peel and dice the other half. Peel, seed, and dice 1 tomato. Dice the apple. Thinly slice the scallion. Combine all these ingredients with the salmon. Season with salt and pepper and mix thoroughly. Cover and chill.

- Boil the fish stock in a small saucepan until reduced to approximately 2 tablespoons. Cool. Snip the chives and stir into the stock. Add the crème fraîche. Season with salt and pepper. Cover and chill.

- Halve the reserved piece of cucumber lengthwise. Scoop out the seeds and slice thinly crosswise. Cut the remaining tomato into 12 wedges.

- To serve, mound the salmon mixture onto salad plates. Spoon the sauce around each serving and garnish with cucumber slices and tomato wedges.

Yield: 4 servings

Gently heat this salad and toss it with linguine in a warm bowl to serve as an entrée.

This salad is also a satisfying luncheon entrée served with bread or muffins and fresh fruit.

Duivekater
(Holiday Sweet Bread)

2 teaspoons dried yeast or 1 ounce
baker's yeast

1 cup plus 3 tablespoons milk,
warmed

3⅓ cups flour

¼ cup sugar

1 teaspoon salt

1 tablespoon grated lemon zest

2 tablespoons butter, softened

1 egg

- Dissolve the yeast in the warm milk. Sift the flour into a large mixing bowl. Make a well in the center and add the milk mixture, working it into about a third of the flour. Add the sugar, salt, lemon zest, and butter. Knead the dough until smooth and elastic. Form into a ball, cover, and let rise in a warm place until doubled.

- Preheat oven to 350°. Punch down the dough and form into a long, oblong loaf. Make a lengthwise cut about 2 inches long through each end of the loaf. Cover with a clean dish towel and let proof for 15 minutes. Make several diagonal slashes across the top of the loaf. Beat the egg with a little water and brush over the loaf.

- Bake on a greased baking sheet for 20 minutes. Reduce heat to 300° and continue baking for 15 minutes. Remove loaf to a wire rack and cool. Slice thinly and serve with butter.

Yield: 1 loaf

In the Netherlands, Duivekater is associated with the feast of Saint Nicholas and is traditionally served from his feast day on December 6 through Epiphany on January 6.

Aardappelpannekoekjes
(Potato Pancakes)

1 cup milk

2 cups cooked, mashed potatoes

1 cup biscuit baking mix

2 tablespoons vegetable oil

2 eggs

Oil for frying

- Combine milk, potatoes, baking mix, vegetable oil, and eggs in a medium bowl and mix well.

- Heat an electric frying pan to 350° or a skillet over medium-high heat with just enough oil to cover the bottom. Drop spoonfuls of batter into the pan and cook 2 to 3 minutes on each side, or until golden brown. Keep warm in the oven until ready to serve.

Yield: 15 to 20 small pancakes

Contributor: Laura Perkins

The batter may be prepared ahead of time and cooked up to 1 hour before serving.

Served with Winter Vegetable Sauce, these pancakes are delicious alongside roasted meat or sausage. They may also be served with butter and preserves as a brunch entrée.

Saus van Wintergroente
(Winter Vegetable Sauce)

2 tablespoons butter

2 ounces bacon, chopped

1 shallot, chopped

1 clove garlic, minced

¼ cup chopped carrots

¼ cup chopped celeriac (celery root)

¼ cup sliced leeks

½ pound mushrooms, chopped

1 cup beef broth

1 tablespoon black currant jelly

Salt and freshly ground pepper

1 tablespoon chopped fresh parsley

- Melt butter over medium heat. Sauté the bacon, shallot, garlic, carrots, celeriac, and leeks until the bacon is just done. Add the mushrooms and continue to sauté for 3 to 4 more minutes.

- Add the broth and jelly and simmer for 10 minutes. Season with salt and pepper. Sprinkle parsley over all. Serve with Potato Pancakes.

Yield: 6 servings

Celery may be substituted for celeriac.

This colorful and flavorful sauce may also be served with baked potatoes to complement a meal of roasted meat.

Kaneel Stoofpeertjes
(Cinnamon Stewed Pears)

2 pounds firm cooking pears

1 cup water

2 tablespoons sugar

½ cinnamon stick

Ground cinnamon

- Peel, halve, and core the pears. In a saucepan, combine pears, water, sugar, and cinnamon stick. Bring to a boil. Cover and simmer gently for about 3 hours or until the pears are soft and reddish brown in color.

- Remove the cinnamon stick. Use a large slotted spoon to lift the pears out into a serving dish. Reduce the cooking liquid until it is slightly thickened. Pour over the pears. Sprinkle with a little ground cinnamon. Serve warm.

Yield: 6 servings

Substituting canned pears will result in a sweeter dish. Use two 16-ounce cans of pear halves packed in natural fruit juice, drained; reduce sugar and cooking time by half.

Cinnamon Stewed Pears complement roasted meats or fish.

Citroentaart met Aardbeien

(Lemon Tart with Strawberries)

Pastry

⅓ cup butter, softened

¼ cup sugar

1 egg

1 cup flour

Pinch of salt

- Cream the butter and sugar. Add the egg and beat thoroughly. Sift the flour and salt into the egg mixture. Mix just until the dough forms a ball. Wrap in plastic wrap and refrigerate for 30 minutes.

- Preheat oven to 400°. Roll out pastry on a lightly floured surface to line the base and sides of a tart pan. Let rest for 15 minutes. Bake the empty pastry shell for about 15 minutes or until very lightly browned. Cool.

Filling and Topping

1 heaping teaspoon cornstarch

½ cup plus 2 tablespoons plain yogurt

2 eggs

½ cup castor sugar

Zest of one lemon

Juice of one lemon

½ cup strawberries

3 tablespoons red currant jelly

Fresh mint sprigs

- Reduce oven temperature to 350°. Stir the cornstarch into the yogurt. Beat together the yogurt mixture, eggs, and sugar until smooth. Stir in the lemon zest and juice. Pour the filling into the precooked pastry shell and bake for 20 minutes. Cool. Remove the cooled tart from the tart pan and transfer to a serving plate.

- Hull and halve the strawberries. Arrange the strawberry halves on top of the tart filling. Melt the jelly in a small saucepan or in the microwave. Brush over the strawberries. Garnish with mint sprigs.

Yield: 8 to 10 servings

Castor sugar is available in specialty markets featuring imported foods; you may substitute fine sugar.

Substitute other fresh fruits such as kiwi slices or whole raspberries for the strawberries, or arrange a variety of fresh fruits on top for a multicolored dessert.

Gentlemen's
Literary Luncheon

— Lavender Room —

Gentlemen's Literary Luncheon
— *Lavender Room* —

Menu

Catfish with Black Walnuts

Roast Haunch of Venison

Mashed Potatoes and Carrots

Asparagus with Walnuts

Baking Powder Biscuits

Strawberry Ice

Sauerkraut Cream Pie

MENU CHAIRMAN:	**CHEF:**
Robert F. Kendall, Friend of the Taft Museum	Jeff Thomas

Jeff Thomas is owner of Jeff Thomas Catering, based in Northern Kentucky, and is remembered for his association with the R.S.V.P. Room in downtown Cincinnati as well as Annie's Pub in the suburb of Wyoming. He is a generous supporter of the arts and numerous charity events. Chef Thomas was assisted in this menu by Chef Paula Kirk, owner of Paula's Gourmet; Todd Westermeyer, apprentice chef with Jean-Robert de Caval, The Maisonette; Mary Reese Gilbert, assistant to Ethan Becker for *The New Joy of Cooking;* and Charles Adams, lover of great food.

John Singer Sargent (American, 1856–1925), *Robert Louis Stevenson,* **1887, oil on canvas, h. 20¹⁄₁₆ x w. 24⁵⁄₁₆. Bequest of Mr. and Mrs. Charles Phelps Taft**

*M*any an interesting luncheon companion graces the Lavender Room. Along with works by artists of literary bent including James A. McNeill Whistler, Sir Lawrence Alma-Tadema, Mariano Fortuny i Marsal, and Jean-Auguste-Dominique Ingres, the portrait of Robert Louis Stevenson by John Singer Sargent plays host to this literary lunch. A sickly child and tubercular adult, Stevenson (English, 1850–1894) nonetheless lived adventurously and traveled widely. He became famous for such tales as *Treasure Island, Kidnapped,* and *The Strange Case of Dr. Jekyll and Mr. Hyde.* Join him and his companions for this culinary adventure featuring foods indigenous to early Cincinnati.

The Literary Life

Martin Baum, the builder of Belmont, inaugurated its reputation as a locus for the literati. "Among many other activities Baum was a founder of the literary society (1818) . . . . If we consider that he was in those days the wealthiest and most respected citizen of the town; that he was also president of the Cincinnati Branch of the Bank of the United States; and that he stood in connection with the most important men of the land, it is clear that Baum was to the German element in the first period a powerful support. His house, the most elegant in the town, was open to all intellectually great men who visited Cincinnati, and German literary men were especially welcome" (Ford, p. 127).

Nicholas Longworth continued that association through his involvement with the Literary Club, while David Sinton built a publishing empire that was eventually taken over by his son-in-law, Charles Phelps Taft.

"Charles, in association with Sinton, had bought the controlling interest in the Cincinnati *Times.* They then absorbed the *Evening Star,* thereby creating a powerful afternoon paper, the *Times-Star,* that was to remain in the family until the 1950's. . . . Charles occupied the editorial chair at the *Times-Star* and in the course of time Annie fell into the habit of making daily trips to the office to act as unofficial adviser" (Ross, p. 66).

Alphonso Taft wrote to his son William Howard on July 2, 1879, urging him to consider a career with the family newspaper. The elder Taft was pleased with Charles's entrance into the world of journalism and felt that other members of the family had an obligation to contribute to it and thereby to add to the community betterment as well (Ross, p. 67).

Upon the death of her father, Annie gave Charles "all of her father's interest in the *Times-Star,* including the stock, the land, and the building. It seemed to Annie that this was Charles's true field and that he ought to be in full possession of the newspaper interests. Young Hulbert Taft joined the paper at about this time, beginning as a reporter. His uncle Charles told him that he would have to work his way up" (Ross, p. 137).

David Sinton, **print. Collection of Cincinnati Museum Center, no. B-93-208**

Catfish with Black Walnuts

Fish

6 fresh catfish fillets

4 cups milk

3 tablespoons kosher or sea salt

2 tablespoons white pepper

1 teaspoon hot pepper sauce

Black Walnut Flour

2 cups finely ground black walnuts

1½ cups yellow cornmeal

½ cup all-purpose flour

2 tablespoons kosher or sea salt

1 teaspoon freshly ground black pepper

1 tablespoon butter

1 cup olive oil

Sauce

½ pound butter, cut into pieces

2 cups chopped black walnuts

Juice of 3 lemons

1 cup chopped fresh parsley

2 tablespoons kosher or sea salt

1 teaspoon freshly ground black pepper

6 lemon wedges

Parsley sprigs

- Rinse fillets and soak overnight in milk, salt, pepper, and hot pepper sauce.

- Mix all dry ingredients for the black walnut flour well. Heat butter and oil until very hot, then reduce heat to medium-high. Dredge fillets in flour mixture and cook until golden brown on both sides. Drain on paper towels and keep warm in 350° oven until all are done.

- To make sauce, remove excess oil from pan. Add butter and brown the black walnuts. Add lemon juice, parsley, salt, and pepper and cook, stirring, for 3 minutes.

- To serve, place one catfish fillet on each plate and spoon sauce across the center. Garnish with a lemon wedge and parsley sprigs.

Yield: 6 servings

You may reduce the amount of salt used throughout this recipe.

Even if you think you don't like catfish, you will enjoy this savory, nutty dish, which is excellent served with greens, spinach, or bok choy.

Roast Haunch of Venison

6 to 7 pound haunch of venison

2 gallons red table wine

3 carrots, finely chopped

3 large onions, finely chopped

5 whole cloves

½ teaspoon each marjoram, thyme, basil, and tarragon

4 tablespoons butter

2 (12- to 16-ounce) packages salt pork, cut into strips

Salt and pepper

Sauce

2 cups red table wine

2 cups red currant jelly

¼ teaspoon ground ginger

¼ teaspoon ground cloves

- In a large bowl or crock, cover venison with red wine. Sauté carrots, onions, cloves, and herbs in butter until vegetables are soft. Pour vegetable mixture over venison. Cover and refrigerate 24 hours, turning occasionally.

- Bring venison to room temperature in marinade, about 8 hours. Preheat oven to 450°. Remove venison from marinade and place on a roasting rack. Cover the venison with all the strips of salt pork, securing ends with toothpicks. Salt and pepper generously. Pour all the marinade into the bottom of the roasting pan. Bake at 450° for 30 minutes. Reduce heat to 350° and cover venison loosely with foil. Roast for 8 hours, removing foil after the first 5 hours, until tender. Add water to the roasting pan as needed to maintain a ½-inch depth of liquid.

- Just before the meat is finished, begin the sauce preparation. Place wine, jelly, ginger, and cloves in a saucepan. Remove meat from oven and strain pan juices into the saucepan. Boil until thickened and reduced by about half, about 10 to 15 minutes.

- Carve the venison as thinly as possible across the grain. Serve with sauce.

Yield: 12 servings

When ordering venison from the butcher, ask for a haunch that has been cured at least 7 days.

You may substitute a beef roast for the venison, adjusting the roasting time as needed.

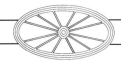
Mashed Potatoes and Carrots

1½ pounds potatoes, quartered

1 pound carrots

½ cup heavy cream

1 egg yolk

¼ pound butter

1 teaspoon prepared mustard

Salt and pepper

- Cook potatoes and carrots separately in boiling water until tender. Drain well and press each through a ricer. Combine the two purées in a large saucepan. Stir in cream, egg yolk, and butter. Season with mustard, salt, and pepper. Heat gently, stirring, and serve hot.

Yield: 10 servings

This sweet purée is a colorful alternative to plain mashed potatoes.

Asparagus with Walnuts

1½ pounds trimmed fresh asparagus

1 cup finely chopped walnuts

2 tablespoons walnut or sesame oil

¼ cup cider vinegar

¼ cup soy or tamarind sauce

⅓ cup sugar

Freshly ground pepper

- Boil asparagus in water to cover until tender-crisp, about 5 to 7 minutes. Drain well. Arrange in a serving dish.

- Combine walnuts, oil, vinegar, soy or tamarind sauce, and sugar. Whisk well to blend. Pour over asparagus. Dust with pepper. Chill. Mix well again before serving.

Yield: 6 servings

Baking Powder Biscuits

4 tablespoons unsalted butter

2 cups all-purpose flour

1 tablespoon baking powder

1 teaspoon salt

¾ cup milk

- Preheat oven to 450°. In a food processor, thoroughly blend the butter, flour, baking powder, and salt until the mixture resembles coarse cornmeal. Add milk and process just until the dough begins to mass together; do not overblend.

- Turn the dough out onto a lightly floured surface and knead briefly. On a clean, floured surface roll the dough ½ inch thick. Cut into 2-inch rounds. Arrange the biscuits on a greased baking sheet and bake for 12 minutes or until golden brown. Serve immediately.

Yield: 10 biscuits

You may need to add a little more milk to form the dough in the food processor.

These biscuits are wonderful for soaking up rich, savory sauces. They are equally good with country ham.

Strawberry Ice

2¾ cups puréed fresh or unsweetened frozen strawberries

2 tablespoons lemon juice

⅔ cup simple syrup (recipe below)

Simple Syrup

2 cups very cold water

2 cups sugar

- Blend strawberry purée, lemon juice, and syrup in food processor or blender. If desired, strain to remove seeds. Pour mixture into an electric ice cream maker and churn until firm, about 15 minutes. Serve at once.

- In a saucepan, blend water and sugar. Bring to a simmer, stirring until sugar is dissolved. Cool to room temperature.

Yield: 10 servings

Strawberry Ice may be served as a dessert or as a palate cleanser between the fish and main courses.

Sauerkraut Cream Pie

Pastry for 2 (9-inch) single pie crusts

½ **cup fresh sauerkraut**

½ **cup butter, softened**

2 cups sugar

5 eggs, well beaten

1 cup milk

1 teaspoon vanilla extract

2 tablespoons fresh lemon juice

2 tablespoons yellow cornmeal

2 tablespoons all-purpose flour

- Preheat oven to 350°. Roll out pastry on a floured surface and line 2 9-inch pie plates; set aside.

- Drain the sauerkraut and rinse well two times. Squeeze dry and set aside.

- In a mixing bowl, cream the butter and sugar thoroughly, about 1 minute. Add the eggs, milk, vanilla, and lemon juice and blend. Combine the flour and cornmeal. Add the flour mixture to the egg mixture and blend. Fold in the sauerkraut.

- Pour into the unbaked pie shells. Bake for 55 to 60 minutes or until a knife inserted in the center comes out clean. Cool completely before cutting and serving.

Yield: 2 9-inch pies

The sauerkraut must be rinsed thoroughly, or it will impart a vinegar flavor to the pie.

Your guests will never guess the secret ingredient in this delicious pie unless you tell them.

Time for Small Treats

A Children's Tea Party

— *Keystone Gallery* —

Time for Small Treats
A Children's Tea Party
— *Keystone Gallery* —

Menu

Cream Cheese and Jelly Fingers
Peanut Butter and Banana Pinwheels
Turkey Heart Sandwiches
Carrot and Celery Sticks

Chocolate Dipped Fruit

Animal Cookies
Lemon Sunshine Cookies

Pink Lemonade

MENU CHAIRWOMAN:
Fran Goldman, Taft Museum Docent

CHEFS:
Sharon Butler and Megan Balterman

In 1983 Sharon Butler founded The Bonbonerie, selling pastries to Cincinnati-area restaurants before opening the current retail establishment four years later. Previously, she had studied painting at Columbia College of Art and Design and holds a degree in fine arts from the University of Cincinnati College of Design, Architecture, Art, and Planning. At the time she helped develop this menu, Megan Balterman was in charge of the tea room at The Bonbonerie, where she continues to work in the bakery and at the counter.

Enameled Varicolored Gold Watch Set
with Diamonds, Quarter Repeating à Toc, **France,**
about 1762–68, diam. 1⅝ in. Bequest of
Mr. and Mrs. Charles Phelps Taft

Children and adults alike marvel at the tiny treasures contained in the Keystone Gallery. There, in the Wadsworth Watch Case, is a veritable treasury of gold, silver, crystal, diamonds, and other precious materials on boxes, plaques, and watches dating from the Renaissance to the 19th century. It is the watches, in particular, that attract comment, speaking of times past through their beautiful crafts-manship and exquisite ornament. Such tiny treasures reward close looking. This small gallery is as full of surprises as the small guests who will eagerly partake of this delicious tea party.

A Home for Children

Children have always played a part in the story of the house on Pike Street. When Martin Baum lived in the house in the first half of the 1820s, he had six children: Jacob, Martin, Mary, David, Kerschner, and Eleanor. For a short time following the Baums' residency, the rooms echoed with the sounds of school girls' recitations. Mrs. Ann Wood leased the house and operated Belmont House, a school for young ladies. By 1830, however, it was again a private home when the Longworths moved in.

Nicholas and Susan Longworth were the parents of four children: Mary, Eliza, Catherine, and Joseph. As each child married, the spouse was brought to live at Belmont as well, and all the Longworths' grandchildren were born there. At one time fourteen grandchildren, eight adults, and various live-in servants all resided in the house (Boehle, p. 17).

We find written in the folio volume *Memorial of the Golden Wedding of Nicholas Longworth and Susan Longworth, Celebrated at Cincinnati on Christmas Eve, 1857,* the following rumination on children and grandchildren:

Children are fruit, grandchildren flowers,

Of matrimony's sun and showers.

Children confer a deep delight,

But keep you much awake at night.

Grandchildren you may pet and spoil,

And leave their parents all the toil.

Although Anna Sinton was already a young lady when her father purchased Belmont, she and her husband, Charles Phelps Taft, raised two sons and two daughters there: Jane, David, Anna Louise, and Howard. In addition, Anna was a doting aunt. When William Howard and Nellie Taft traveled, their children were welcome guests. And even Charles's younger brothers found a second home there. Anna was noted for serving delicious meals and providing "concert tickets as well as beefsteak" (Ross, pp. 89–90).

Unidentified children from *Memorial of the Golden Wedding of Nicholas Longworth and Susan Longworth, Celebrated at Cincinnati on Christmas Eve, 1857,* lithograph

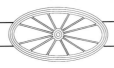

Cream Cheese and Jelly Fingers

2 slices white sandwich bread

1 tablespoon cream cheese, softened

1½ teaspoons grape jelly

- Spread cream cheese on one slice of bread. Spread jelly over cream cheese. Top with second slice of bread. Refrigerate half an hour.

- With a serrated knife, remove bread crusts. Slice in half lengthwise, and slice each half lengthwise again to make 4 fingers.

Yield: 4 finger sandwiches

Arrange Cream Cheese and Jelly Fingers, Peanut Butter and Banana Pinwheels, and Turkey Heart Sandwiches on a pretty plate, garnished with carrot and celery sticks cut with decorative cutters.

Peanut Butter and Banana Pinwheels

1 slice whole wheat sandwich bread

2 tablespoons smooth peanut butter

1 small banana

- Trim crusts from the slice of bread. Use a rolling pin to flatten it slightly to about ¼ inch. Spread with peanut butter.

- Peel banana and trim off ends to leave a central piece the length of the bread slice. Place banana at edge of the bread and roll so that bread is wrapped around the banana. Refrigerate ½ hour.

- Trim ends of the roll and cut into ½-inch slices.

Yield: 6 pinwheels

Lightly brush the tops of the cut bananas with lemon juice to prevent them from browning unless serving immediately.

This is a common snack and children's party offering in Northern Ontario.

Turkey Heart Sandwiches

2 slices white sandwich bread

2 tablespoons mayonnaise

2 slices turkey breast

- Spread each slice of bread with mayonnaise. Place turkey slices on one slice of bread and top with second slice.
- Use a 2-inch heart-shaped cookie cutter to cut out 4 heart sandwiches.

Yield: 4 sandwiches

Look for large, square slices of bread, or you will get fewer hearts from each whole sandwich.

Chocolate Dipped Fruit

White Chocolate Grapes

8 ounces green grapes

4 ounces white chocolate

- Wash grapes and dry thoroughly. Cut bunches into small clusters of 4 to 6 grapes.
- Melt chocolate in a glass bowl in the microwave or on top of a double boiler over boiling water. Dip each cluster into melted chocolate. Place on a plate or tray covered with waxed paper. Refrigerate until chocolate is set.

Milk Chocolate Strawberries

4 large strawberries

4 ounces milk chocolate

- Wash and dry strawberries thoroughly. Melt chocolate in a glass bowl in the microwave or on top of a double boiler over boiling water. Dip each strawberry halfway into melted chocolate. Place on a plate or tray covered with waxed paper. Refrigerate until chocolate is set.
- To serve, alternate grape clusters and strawberries on a plate covered with a paper doily.

Yield: 4 servings

Animal Cookies

4 ounces butter, softened

¾ cup sugar

1 egg

½ teaspoon vanilla

1¼ cups flour

⅛ teaspoon salt

¼ teaspoon baking powder

½ teaspoon cinnamon

½ teaspoon cloves

½ teaspoon nutmeg

Egg wash (one beaten egg white)

Multicolored nonpareils or sugar crystals

- Cream butter and sugar. Beat in the egg and vanilla. Sift together flour, salt, baking powder, cinnamon, cloves, and nutmeg. Stir dry ingredients into butter mixture. Wrap dough in plastic wrap and chill thoroughly.

- Preheat oven to 350°. Roll dough to ⅛ inch thick. Use cookie cutters to cut into animal shapes. Place on greased or parchment-lined cookie sheets. Brush with egg wash and sprinkle with nonpareils or sugar crystals. Bake approximately 10 minutes or until lightly browned.

Yield: 2 dozen cookies

These cookies—cut into flowers, stars, or hearts and with or without the nonpareils—are equally delicious for adult tea parties.

Lemon Sunshine Cookies

½ **pound butter, softened**

1 **cup sugar**

2 **eggs**

¾ **teaspoon vanilla**

Zest from three quarters of a lemon

1½ **cups flour**

¼ **teaspoon salt**

- Preheat oven to 375°. Cream butter and sugar until fluffy. Beat in eggs, vanilla, and lemon zest. Stir in flour and salt.
- Use a spoon or a pastry bag with a medium round tip to make 2-inch oblongs onto a greased or parchment-lined cookie sheet. Bake approximately 10 minutes or until edges are brown.

Yield: 90 2-inch cookies

You will want to make these simple, delicious cookies again . . . and again and again.

Pink Lemonade

1 **(6-ounce) can frozen lemonade concentrate**

2 **tablespoons raspberry or strawberry syrup**

- Prepare lemonade according to package directions. Add raspberry or strawberry syrup. Serve from a china teapot into teacups.

Yield: 32 ounces

Fruit-flavored herbal tea or commercial pink lemonade are also good beverage choices for this children's party.

Fête Champêtre

A Country Picnic

— Garden —

Fête Champêtre
A Country Picnic
— Garden —

Menu

Hors d'Oeuvre
Cantaloupe and Ham Wraps

Main Event
The Big Sandwich
Garden Tortellini Salad
Rosebud Beet Salad

Dessert
Oatmeal Pecan Wafers
Fresh Whole Strawberries with Powdered Sugar for Dipping

MENU CHAIRWOMAN:
Barbara Kiefer, Taft Museum Docent

Barbara Kiefer conceived a menu that is both portable and delicious. Serve it in your own garden or carry it to the country, a park, or a potluck buffet. In honor of Nicholas Longworth's prize crops, don't forget the champagne and strawberries for dessert.

120

Garden of the Taft Museum

*E*ven before the house was built on the property Martin Baum purchased near Deer Creek, he laid out a garden there. The next resident, Nicholas Longworth, was also an avid gardener, cultivating grapes and strawberries as well as trees and flowers. Although we find no mention of the grounds during the Sinton or Taft residencies, today the formal garden is the site of Museum functions and private parties, echoing with the joyful sounds of fêtes both past and present.

Baum's Folly, or the Garden of Eden

"Baum's Folly" was what people called the mansion being built by Martin Baum in the early 1820s, because the city and country were struck by a financial panic at the time. Earlier, however, the citizens had enjoyed wandering through the gardens that Baum had developed on the property. One garden stood where the Taft Museum is located on the west bank of Deer Creek. The other, on the east bank, was planted by Johannes Staubler, a German immigrant. "Take this land and make a garden on it," Baum had instructed him. Baum's garden soon became the showplace of the city and the first "art garden" and vineyard in the Northwest Territory. Unfortunately, Baum fell prey to the financial crisis, resulting in the house and property being deeded to the Bank of the United States in 1825 (Ott, n.p.).

In 1838 Harriet Martineau, a visitor to Cincinnati, wrote of a visit to Nicholas Longworth's garden: "The proprietor has a passion for gardening, and his ruling taste seems likely to be a blessing to the city. He employs four gardeners, and toils in his grounds with his own hands. His garden is on a terrace which overlooks a canal, and the most parklike eminences form the background of the view. Between the garden and the hills extend his vineyards, from the produce of which he has succeeded in making twelve kinds of wine, some of which are highly praised by good judges. Mr. Longworth himself is sanguine as to the prospect of making Ohio a wine growing region, and he has done all that an individual can to enhance the probability" (Taft Museum, n.p.).

Longworth's gardener, a Mr. Adlum, came upon a grapevine growing in Longworth's experimental vineyards near Vevay, Indiana. From that single plant of unknown origin, grapes were developed for sparkling Catawba wine, which became a popular brand in America and Europe. All the hillsides to Mt. Adams as far as Mt. Lookout were eventually planted with Catawba grapes. Longworth thought of those vineyards as his "Garden of Eden" (Boehle, pp. 15–16). Appropriately, much of that land is now Eden Park, an extraordinary gift to the community from an extraordinary man.

Title page from the *Memorial of the Golden Wedding of Nicholas Longworth and Susan Longworth Celebrated at Cincinnati on Christmas Eve, 1857*, lithograph

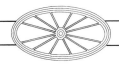

Cantaloupe and Ham Wraps

1 ripe cantaloupe, peeled, sliced, and cubed

3 to 4 thin slices deli baked ham

- Cut ham slices into strips. Wrap one strip around each melon cube and fix with an hors d'oeuvre pick. Serve at room temperature.

Yield: 30 pieces

Prosciutto may be substituted for the ham if it is sliced as close as possible to serving time and stored in a dark, airtight container until served.

This hors d'oeuvre is simple, colorful, and elegant.

The Big Sandwich

1 oblong loaf Vienna-style bread

⅓ cup Italian dressing

6 to 8 leaves fresh spinach, stems removed

1 cup grated mozzarella cheese, divided use

1 small red onion, thinly sliced

6 to 8 slices roast turkey breast

1 small tomato, thinly sliced

1 small cucumber, thinly sliced

6 large stuffed green olives, sliced

- Preheat oven to 350°. Slice top third from the loaf of bread. Remove enough of the soft center of the top and bottom to leave a ½-inch shell.
- Lightly brush the inside of the shells with dressing. Inside the bottom shell, layer spinach, ½ cup cheese, onion, turkey, tomato, cucumber, and olives. Top with remaining cheese and replace top of loaf.
- Wrap sandwich in foil. Bake 35 to 40 minutes. Cool 10 minutes. Cut into 2-inch slices. Serve hot or cold.

Yield: 4 to 6 servings

To make individual sandwiches, use 4 hoagie-style sandwich rolls and bake 25 to 30 minutes.

123

Garden Tortellini Salad

1 (7- to 8-ounce) box dried tortellini

Olive oil

½ cup bottled Caesar salad dressing

1 to 2 cloves garlic, crushed

Juice of 1 to 2 lemons

1 red bell pepper, diced

1 yellow or green bell pepper, diced

1 (16-ounce) can artichoke hearts,
    halved

¾ cup grated fresh Parmesan cheese

Salt and pepper

- Cook tortellini according to package directions. Drain well. Toss with a little olive oil in a large glass bowl. Cool.

- Whisk together salad dressing, garlic, and lemon juice. Add dressing mixture and the remaining ingredients to the tortellini and toss well. Refrigerate at least 4 hours before serving.

Yield: 8 servings

Contributor: Laura Wild Conover

This salad keeps well in the refrigerator for several days.

Garden Tortellini Salad, fruit, crusty bread, and perhaps a bottle of chilled white wine are all you need for a light summer meal. Made with red and green bell peppers, it is also perfect on your holiday buffet.

Rosebud Beet Salad

1 (13½-ounce) can rosebud, or small whole, beets

¼ cup white vinegar

½ cup reserved beet juice

2 tablespoons sugar

2 whole cloves

½ teaspoon salt

3 whole peppercorns

2 hard cooked eggs, coarsely chopped

2 tablespoons coarsely chopped sweet onion

¼ cup reduced fat mayonnaise

- Drain beets, reserving liquid. Place in a glass jar. In a small saucepan, bring vinegar and ½ cup beet juice to a boil. Add sugar, cloves, salt, and peppercorns and stir to dissolve until mixture returns to a boil. Pour liquid over the beets. Cover and chill for several hours or overnight.

- Drain beets and remove cloves and peppercorns. Combine with chopped eggs, onion, and mayonnaise. Serve chilled.

Yield: 4 to 6 servings

To substitute prepared pickled beets, simply combine drained beets with eggs, onion, and mayonnaise.

The brilliant red of this salad is perfectly complemented when it is served on a lettuce leaf.

125

Oatmeal Pecan Wafers

1 cup butter, softened

1 cup brown sugar

2 eggs, beaten

1 teaspoon vanilla

1½ cups sifted flour

1 teaspoon salt

1 teaspoon baking soda

3 cups quick oats

½ cup chopped pecans

- Cream butter and sugar. Beat in eggs and vanilla. Add dry ingredients and nuts. Mix well. Form into three rolls. Wrap in plastic wrap and chill thoroughly.

- Preheat oven to 350°. Slice rolls into ¼- to ⅜-inch thick wafers. Bake on lightly greased cookie sheets for 10 to 12 minutes.

Yield: approximately 40 cookies

You may substitute walnuts for the pecans.

Unbaked rolls may be refrigerated for up to 10 days or frozen.

Sources Cited

Atlantic Monthly   Atlantic Monthly, *Cincinnati*, vol. XX, Boston, 1867.

Boehle   Rose Angela Boehle, *Maria*, Dayton, OH, 1990.

Brockwell   Maurice W. Brockwell, *A Catalogue of the Paintings in the Collection of Mr. and Mrs. Charles P. Taft at Cincinnati, Ohio*, New York, 1920.

Cary   F. C. Cary, ed., *The Cincinnatus*, vol. I, College Hill, OH, 1857.

Chambrun, *Cincinnati*   Clara de Chambrun, *Cincinnati: The Story of the Queen City*, New York, 1939.

Chambrun, *Longworth*   Clara de Chambrun, *The Making of Nicholas Longworth*, New York, 1933.

Duffy   Herbert S. Duffy, *William Howard Taft*, New York, 1930.

Ford   Henry A. Ford and Kate B. Ford, *History of Cincinnati*, Cincinnati, 1881.

Ott   Marilyn Z. Ott, "Martin Baum," unpublished ms., Taft Museum archives, 1975.

Ross   Ishbel Ross, *An American Family*, Cleveland, 1964.

Taft Museum   "The Taft Museum," reprint from *The Bulletin of the Cincinnati Art Museum*, Jan. 1933.

WPA   WPA Writers' Program, *Cincinnati*, Cincinnati, 1943.

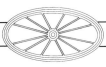

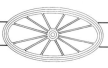

VENISON

W

Z

ZUCCHINI

Notes

Notes

TAFT MUSEUM

316 Pike Street

Cincinnati, OH 45202

Fax: (513) 241-2266

Please send _____ copies of *The Perfect Setting:*
Menus and Memories from Cincinnati's Taft Museum .... @ $21.95 each _____

Gift wrapping: .... @ $ 2.00 each _____

Ohio residents add 6% sales tax .... _____

Shipping and handling (one copy): .... @ $ 5.00 _____

Shipping (two copies to the same address): .... @ $ 7.00 _____

Total _____

Ship to (no P.O. boxes, please):

Name: _____

Address: _____

City: _____ State: _____ Zip: _____

Daytime telephone: _____

❑ Check enclosed

Please make checks payable to *Taft Museum*

❑ Please charge to: ❑ VISA   ❑ MasterCard

Account number: _____ Expiration date: _____

Signature of cardholder: _____

❑ Please send membership information.

Please allow 4 weeks for delivery.

Wholesale prices available on request. Please call (513) 241-0343, ext. 22.

TAFT MUSEUM

316 Pike Street

Cincinnati, OH 45202

Fax: (513) 241-2266

Please send _____ copies of *The Perfect Setting:*
   Menus and Memories from Cincinnati's Taft Museum .... @ $21.95 each _____

Gift wrapping: .... @ $ 2.00 each _____

Ohio residents add 6% sales tax .... _____

Shipping and handling (one copy): .... @ $ 5.00 _____

Shipping (two copies to the same address): .... @ $ 7.00 _____

Total _____

Ship to (no P.O. boxes, please):

Name: _____

Address: _____

City: _____ State: _____ Zip: _____

Daytime telephone: _____

❑ Check enclosed

   Please make checks payable to *Taft Museum*

❑ Please charge to: ❑ VISA   ❑ MasterCard

Account number: _____ Expiration date: _____

Signature of cardholder: _____

❑ Please send membership information.

Please allow 4 weeks for delivery.

Wholesale prices available on request. Please call (513) 241-0343, ext. 22.